SUPERSTARS

SUPERSTARS

OF THE PREMIER LEAGUE

Author: Jim Drewett

Editors: Peter Higham

Rachael Soar

Design: Karen Bates

A FourFourTwo book

Superstars Of The Premier League

This edition first published by Parragon Book Service Ltd in 1996
Parragon Book Service Ltd
Unit 13-17 Avonbridge Trading Estate
Atlantic Road
Avonmouth
Bristol BS11 9QD
Produced by *FourFourTwo*, Haymarket Magazines Ltd
and Magpie Books Ltd

Cover pictures and illustrations courtesy of Allsport and Tim Healy
Repro by Rodney Howe Ltd
Copyright © Haymarket Magazines Ltd 1996
ISBN 0 75251 857 7

Contents

Age 29

Date of Birth 10.10.66

Place of Birth London

Nickname Rodders [as in the
Only Fools and Horses character]

League Games & Goals
Arsenal 367 [23]

Tony Adams' 1995/96 season
Adams played 22 league games
for Arsenal but, surprisingly,
didn't net a single goal

Honours
Division One Champions
1988/89 & 1990/91
FA Cup 1993
Football League Cup 1987 & 1993
European Cup Winners' Cup 1994

Position/Role
Dying for the cause every
Saturday, arm raised until the last

**Word most often used to describe
him**
Solid

Word never used to describe him
Pansy

> "He's Mr Irreplaceable,
> it's as simple as that."
>
> Frank McLintock

The time has come for re-building at Arsenal. But as Bruce Rioch dons his hard hat and demolition work gets underway at Arsenal, the Gunners' boss will be safe in the knowledge that the foundations for Arsenal's future are already in place – in the shape of Tony Adams.

For while the tabloids are cluttered with names allegedly on the move from north London, the one name never mentioned is that of the Gooners' inspirational centre back. Try to imagine Tony Adams in a Manchester United shirt and you can't do it, your mind draws a blank, because Tony Adams is Arsenal right down to those silly hooped socks, and an Arsenal team without its long-standing skipper is, frankly, inconceivable.

Former Gunners captain Frank McLintock agrees: "He's Mr Irreplaceable, it's as simple as that. You don't find many good captains in the game these days, not people like Dave Mackay, Alan Mullery, Tommy Smith and Billy Bremner. But Tony Adams fits that mould. If he ever wanted to leave Arsenal, and I can't believe in his heart of heart that he ever would, the board should break the bank to keep him. He's a born leader."

Adams' leadership qualities have never been in doubt – just ask Terry Venables – but thanks to the *Daily Mirror*'s graphics department and a few dodgy performances on live TV, the 'donkey' tag has taken a long time to shake off.

"Those things that were said about him, the donkey ears and all that, they just served as a stimulant to him," says Don Howe who was assistant manager at Arsenal in 1984 when Adams made his debut aged just 17. Howe describes him as "a truly great defender. He took it all on the chin and got on with it".

Adams is a product of an Arsenal youth team which included the likes of Paul Merson, Paul Davis, Michael Thomas and David Rocastle, and Howe recalls: "It was a real top notch bunch but Tony was the leader even then." All but Merson have now fled the Arsenal nest, but Arsenal can't bring themselves to imagine that Adams could ever be led astray.

Tony
ADAMS

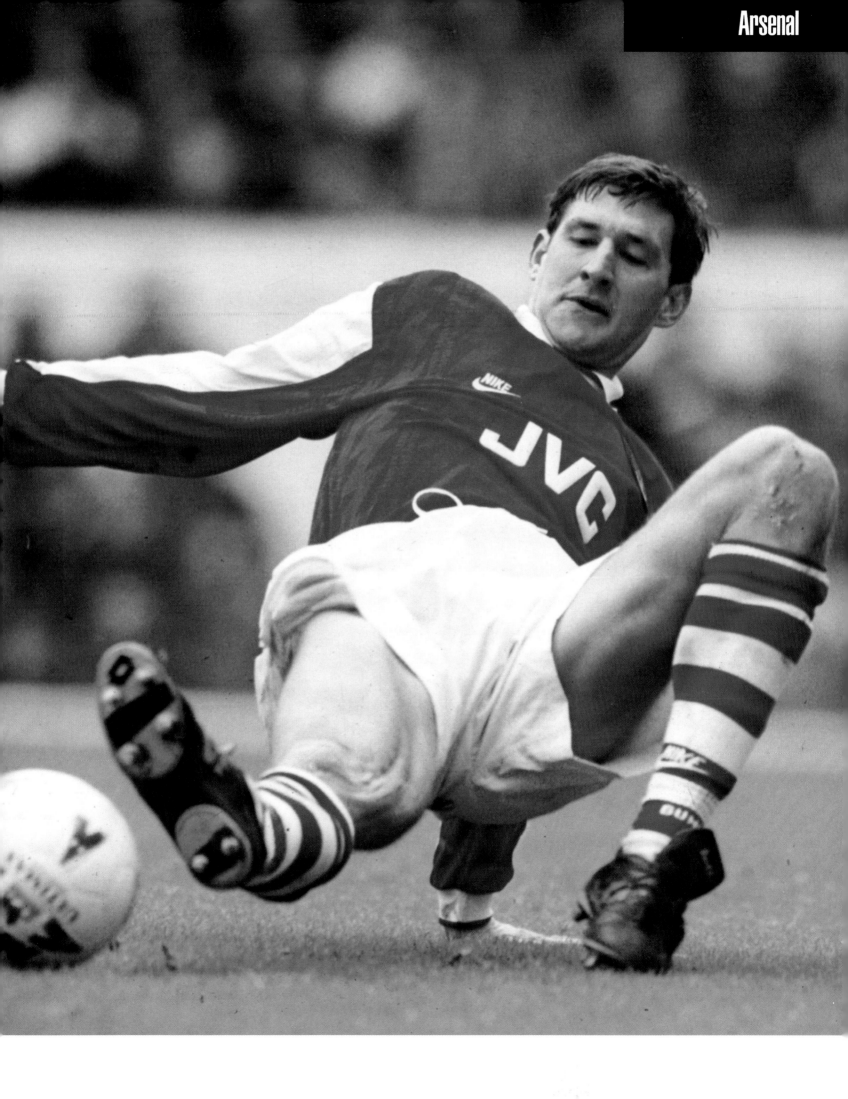

Age 24

Date of Birth 3.3.72

Place of Birth
Southampton

Nickname
Shaggy [after the Scooby Doo character]

League Games & Goals
Portsmouth 62 [6]
Tottenham Hotspur 116 [19]

Darren Anderton's 95/96 season
A nightmare eight league appearances and just two goals thanks to his injury hell. The only silver lining was a return to the England set-up for Euro 96.

Transfers
Portsmouth to Tottenham [£1.75m]

Position/Role
Either darting towards the opposition goal...
or the treatment room

Word most often used to describe him
Dazzling

Word never used to describe him
Chunky

"I'm a real moaner during games, I'm always determined to do well."

Darren Anderton

D arren 'Shaggy' Anderton sometimes looks like the sort of player who never gets picked for park kickarounds. Well, let's face it, he looks so gawky you'd never think he could play football. So maybe defences are fooled into a false sense of security by the Tottenham and England wideboy. With his ruffled hair, beanpole stature and sloping shoulders, Anderton looks like he'd be hard pressed to skin a peach, let alone a top class defender.

Any such thinking by a defender can be filed directly in the wishful section. With a quick shuffle and a turn of pace that puts his Scooby Doo namesake to shame, Anderton can whip past his man and down to the by-line before you can say "don't judge a book by its cover". Even after a disastrous groin-injury-dominated season, which has made the sight of Anderton in the Tottenham line-up about as rare as a Ronnie Rosenthal goal at White Hart Lane, he's still high on the list of the finest attackers in the country.

"He's very deceptive," says his Spurs skipper Gary Mabbutt. "In a way he's like Chris Waddle, in that he looks ungainly yet he's extremely quick. He loves taking people on and beating them and he's one of the best crossers of the ball I've seen in my career. He's also got a lethal shot."

Anderton is the antithesis of the traditional five-foot nothing-sixpence-ha'penny winger, but is hardly built in the manner of a playmaking midfielder either, though he has excelled for Spurs in a central role, drawing comparisons with the old master Sir Glenn himself at the Lane.

Such versatility is the stuff of England managers' dreams, and Anderton looks like he might well figure in the international set-up for some years. Has he found the transition difficult? "It's a totally different game," he says. "It's not necessarily more difficult, though. You're playing against better players, sure, but you're playing with better players, too. I've enjoyed playing with Gazza, Paul Ince, David Platt. They've really brought out the best in me."

Maybe he's right, but let's hope not. Because if it's still to come, we've really something to look forward to.

Darren ANDERTON

Age 26

Date of Birth 10.11.69

Place of Birth Tulua [Columbia]

Nickname Black Gazelle

Clubs
Nacional De Medellin
[Colombia]
Parma [Italy]
Newcastle 14 [3]

International record
Asprilla has played for
Colombia more than 30
times, scoring on nine
occasions

Honours
He has won the Colombian
championship with Nacional
plus the UEFA Cup, European
Cup Winners Cup and Super
Cup with Palma.

Position/Role
Going all rubbery-legged to
bamboozle defenders [as well
as his own team-mates]

**Word most often used to describe
him**
Live-wire

Word never used to describe him
Lethargic

> "There's no one
> like him." Kevin Keegan

t's 4.22pm on Saturday, February 10th, 1996. Newcastle, top of the table, nine points clear with one game in hand, are trailing 1-0 at lowly Middlesbrough with 23 minutes to go. The Teesiders have lost their previous six games and are desperate to get a second clinching goal: they're jabbing away at the Newcastle defence like 11 Barry McGuigans and only desperate finishing from Barmby saves the Geordies from a humiliating derby thrashing.

A loss in Humberside would be a huge body blow to Keegan's men, and he knows it. Newcastle desperately need a fillip and he's sitting on the bench. Faustino Asprilla, all £7.5 million's worth, has flown in from Italy that very morning and, having drunk a pre-match glass of wine, is raring to go, especially as he's freezing his cojones off.

And Middlesbrough fans thought that their South American was good. Asprilla simply takes Bryan Robson's men apart. Almost immediately he sets up Newcastle's equaliser, feinting first one way then the other, the rubbery texture of his legs hypnotising poor Steve Vickers who is used to more staple fare. Then, with a deft flick off the inside of his boot, Asprilla pushes the ball in the other direction, and leaves the full back lurching in no man's land to give him a free run at goal. Seeing Steve Watson lurking at the far post, he jabs over a perfect cross. It's 1-1, and Newcastle has a new hero.

Unfortunately, the fairytale beginning sours pretty quickly. In the 3-3 draw with Man' City, Asprilla scores his first goal for United, but is rather too liberal with his forehead and elbows and has to make a cap-in-hand trip to the FA. He continues to stun spectators with his skills, but he's often two steps ahead of his team-mates and chances go to waste. Newcastle go through a distinctly dodgy patch and his arrival coincides with Manchester United's wresting control of the Premiership steering wheel.

It would be harsh to say that it was the Colombian's fault. What's he supposed to do: play worse? The problem could be that he's simply too good. The man's so unpredictable that it's not just the other team's defenders that don't know what he's going to do next, half the time his own team-mates haven't got a clue either!

Faustino ASPRILLA

Age 22

Date of Birth 11.2.74

Place of Birth Hull

League Games & Goals
Tottenham 87 [20]
Middlesbrough 32 [7]

Best known for
Being the only 'Boro player who has never played for Brazil – apart from Jamie Pollock.

Nicky Barmby's 95/96 season
A stonking start, scoring in his first game at Arsenal.
Played in 32 of 'Boro's 42 league matches and scored seven times. It would've been twice that if he'd carried on like he started.

Transfers
Tottenham to Middlesbrough [£4m]

Position/Role
Young Peter Beardsley

Word most often used to describe him
Rosy

Word[s] never used to describe him
Past it

> **"I just hope the number 7 shirt is as good for Nick as it was for me over the years."**
>
> Bryan Robson

icky Barmby had such a stunning start to the season that they started calling him the new Peter Beardsley. He seemed to have it all – the tenacious tackle, the vision to read other players' runs, the ability to run into space himself, the canny knack of finding the gap between the opposing keeper and his posts. Hell, against the advice of fashion experts the world over, he even started growing himself a Peter Beardsley haircut.

Having snatched him from reluctant-to-sell Tottenham, 'Boro boss Bryan Robson had so much faith in the player that at the start of the season, he handed him his own, treasured, number 7 jersey. "I've had a good run in it. I just hope the shirt is as good for Nick as it was for me over the years," he said.

So when the little Brazilian Juninho arrived on Teeside, with Middlesbrough in a top-half-of-the-table-and-rising position in the Premiership and a packed Riverside Stadium yelling vociferous support to Robson's new-look team, the future looked rosy indeed, as rosy as Barmby's cheeks after a long hard winter game.

Unfortunately life isn't as easy as all that and Barmby, who had until then either had a hand in or scored just about all of Middlesbrough's goals, started fading. Maybe the Brazilian was too similar a player to himself – both of them seem to play better with Craig Hignett – maybe he'd done too much too soon, maybe it was because he changed the Peter Beardsley haircut for a shorter crop.

Suddenly he looked two years younger, and started playing like he'd unlearnt all the stuff that had made him such a great prospect over the past couple of seasons. To make matters worse, Middlesbrough started fading with him, and in the late winter started freefalling dangerously towards the relegation area.

A late run of form, of course, stopped the rot. And Barmby is too good a player to let a bad run of form affect his confidence too much. As with team-mates Branco and Juninho, this season will be crucial to the young forward. A great deal is expected of the England international. Which is just as well, because that's exactly what he's capable of delivering.

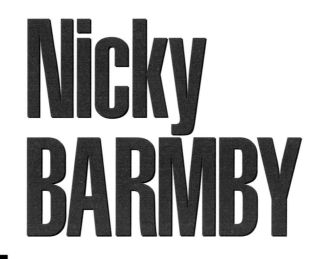

Nicky BARMBY

Age 27

Date of Birth 19.5.69

Place of Birth Amsterdam

Nickname The ice man

League Games & Goals
Ajax [Holland] 185 [85]
Inter Milan [Italy] 52 [11]
Arsenal 33 [11]

Honours
European Cup Winners' Cup
1987 [Ajax], UEFA Cup 1993
[Inter Milan]

Position/Role
On another planet, several light
years from the one Ray Parlour
and David Hillier inhabit.

**Word most often used to describe
him**
Icy

Word never used to describe him
Excitable

> "I always strive for
> perfection in the game.
> No matter what I do I
> know I can do better."
>
> Dennis Bergkamp

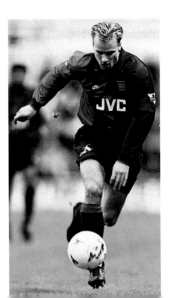

Who's ice cool and red hot all at the same time? Dutch international Dennis Bergkamp, that's who. The Arsenal striker, who hardly breaks into a sweat and never seems to have a hair out of place, may have cost a cool £7.5 million but Arsenal fans reckon he's the bargain of the century.

A creator as well as a scorer of great goals, Bergkamp oozes class from every pore, a pure thoroughbred in a league which some would say is blessed with its fair share of donkeys. With 16 goals to his name last season, Bergkamp can sit back and be more than satisfied with his first season with the Gunners. But will he?

"I always strive for perfection in the game," he says. "No matter what I do I always know I can do better. That's what keeps me going. But if things don't come off there's no point getting annoyed or frustrated. I just bide my time because I know the chance will come again and then I will take it."

The chance to come to England – and pick up £30,000 a week in the process – was one the Dutch number 10 jumped at. After two miserable years floundering in Serie A with Inter Milan, played out of position as an out and out striker instead of in his favoured deeper role, Bergkamp couldn't wait to board the plane and sign for Rioch's Arsenal. At Milan things were so bad at one point, that the other players renamed their 'donkey of the week' award (for the worst player in the previous Sunday's game) to the 'Bergkamp of the Week' award!

So when Arsenal came in for the striker who made his debut for Ajax aged 16 and scored 85 goals in 185 league games for the Dutch giants, he had no hesitation – even though he supported Tottenham as a kid and used to kick a ball around in the park in a Glenn Hoddle shirt. He wanted to play in England, he said, and Arsenal were the first team to ask him.

If you think he's just along for the ride, though, think again. Paul Merson says he always finishes training, gets changed and asks, "Where's Dennis?". The answer, invariably, is he's still out training. Maybe he's in training for the time when Bruce Rioch can provide a few team-mates on the same wavelength. Perhaps then he'll start smiling...

Dennis BERGKAMP

Age 27

Date of Birth 2.6.69

Place of Birth Holland

Clubs
Feyenoord [Holland]
Sheffield Wednesday 9 [2]

Regi Blinker's 1995/96 season
Looked like it was going to be a nightmare after his rows at Feyenoord, but David Pleat rescued his career and Blinker established himself as the fans favourite at Hillsborough

Honours
Dutch League 1993
Dutch Cup 1992, 1994 and 1995

Transfers
Feyenoord to Sheffield Wednesday [£250,000]

Position/Role
Doing his bit for the Wig Marketing Board

Word most often used to describe him
Dreadly

Word never used to describe him
Bald

"When I noticed those kids wearing Regi wigs I was absolutely amazed."

Regi Blinker

f you'd invested your life savings in a company that makes dreadlock wigs this time last year, you might be reading this while sipping chilled champagne on a yacht in the Caribbean. For no sooner had worldwide stocks of dreadlock wigs run out at Gullit-worshipping Stamford Bridge last season, than the Sheffield Wednesday club shop was shifting them as quickly as they could get hold of them to celebrate the arrival of another flying Dutchman, Regi Blinker.

"When I noticed those kids wearing Regi wigs I was absolutely amazed," says Blinker, who returned the compliment with some dazzling wingplay and scorching finishing after his move from Dutch club Feyenoord at the end of last season. "That kind of thing just doesn't happen in Holland."

Well actually the kind of things Blinker's been doing for Wednesday don't exactly happen at Hillsborough much these days either... at least not since Chris Waddle started getting a bit too close to the sell-by date for comfort. "Regi is just like Chris Waddle," enthuses Wednesday's John Sheridan. "He makes magic."

But the most astonishing thing of all is that, in a world of increasingly ludicrous multi-million pound transfer deals, the wizardly wideman cost the club a measly £250,000. Rubbing his hands together, gleeful Wednesday boss David Pleat explains: "Regi had a fall out with the Feyenoord coach and was told that he wouldn't be getting a new contract at the end of the season. Then along came the Bosman case, and Feyenoord knew that they had to take what they could get or lose him for nothing in a couple of months time. Now I think that we have a cult figure in the making. Our fans love him because he excites." And if you did that at Hillsbrough last season, boy did you stand out.

In fact, Blinker's two goals on his debut away to Aston Villa were just about the two most exciting things that happened at Sheffield Wednesday during the whole of last season. David Pleat has some re-building work to do, there's no doubt about that, and that means bringing in some new faces. If the Wednesday fans had their way, not to mention the wig manufacturers, they'd all have dreadlocks!

Regi BLINKER

Vital Statistics

Age 32

Date of Birth 4.4.64

Real Name
Claudio Ibraim Vaz Leal

Why Branco?
'Branco' means white, and he is called it because he was the only white player in his junior team

League Games & Goals [where known]
Fluminese [Brazil]
Genoa [Italy]
Porto [Portugal]
Brescia [Italy]
International [Brazil] 40 [11]
Middlesbrough 7 [0]

Branco's 1995/96 season
Struggled for fitness and didn't even manage a free-kick goal

Appearances for Brazil 83

World Cup Finals Three [1986/90/94]

Position/Role
Very full back, a set-piece cannon

Word most often used to describe him
Hotshot

Word never used to describe him
Thin

> **"I am very happy to be here."** Branco

The Brazilian Player of the Year Juninho's arrival at previously unfashionable Middlesbrough FC was such a big news story, his picture made the front page of all the national papers. When a second Brazilian arrived at the Riverside Stadium a few months later, it only received a few column inches in the sports pages – even though, with 80 caps to his name and a World Cup medal round his neck, Branco had good grounds for claiming to be a far more accomplished player than his whippersnapper young compatriot.

But if the nation as a whole couldn't seem to give a samba about the Branco deal, the good people of Middlesbrough were wildly excited. One Brazilian at 'Boro was as thrill. Two meant Heaven on Earth.

So when Branco was put into the reserve team against Leicester City reserves at the Riverside Stadium to give him a bit of match practice, the start of the game had to be delayed for half an hour – because 15,000 people turned up.

What they saw was an overweight middle-aged-looking guy who couldn't run too fast but could hit the ball incredibly hard. Branco took all the corners and free kicks, and memories of that humdinger of a semifinal winner against Holland in the 1994 World Cup made mid-winter Middlesbrough seem, at times, like the Copa Cobana in August.

Branco made his debut as substitute against Everton, and a daisy-cutting volley that flew two feet off the ground, beat the keeper, but landed in the side netting, promised well for the future.

After such high expectations, disappointment was almost inevitable and lack of fitness and niggling injury meant that the full-back-cum-midfielder was in and out of the side. He was, however, assigned a personal trainer and started noticably shedding the pounds.

His contract, moreover, (a deal that cost Middlesbrough nothing at all in transfer deals but added quite a lump to the wage bill) is for 18 months and quite a bit is expected of the veteran former Genoa player this season. His arrival coincided with a freefall crisis at the Riverside, but if, as expected, the 'Boro can pick up the pieces in August, Branco will be looking to help Bryan Robson's side to a place in Europe. And if they can achieve a few more set pieces in the opposing half, his name might well start appearing at the top of the Goal of the Month charts, too.

BRANCO

Age 30

Date of Birth 24.5.66

Place of Birth
Marseilles, France

League Games & Goals
Auxerre 81 [23]
Marseille 22 [5]
Bordeaux 11 [6]
Montpellier 33 [10]
Marseilles 18 [8]
Nimes 17 [2]
Leeds Utd 28 [9]
Manchester Utd 107 [53]

Honours
French Championship
(Marseilles) 1990/91.
First Division Championship
[Leeds] 1991/92.
Premiership 1992/93,
1993/94, 1995/96.
FA Cup 1994, 1996.

Transfers
Auxerre to Marseilles
[£2.2m]
Bordeaux [loan]
Marseilles to Nimes [£1m]
Nimes to Leeds [£900,000]
Leeds to Man Utd [£1.2m]

Position/Role
Making crowds go
'ooh la la!'

Word most often used to describe him
Un-brie-lievable

Word never used to describe him
Magnifique

"I am happy I stayed."

Eric Cantona

t's not fair. Manchester United have a distinct advantage over other teams. They've 'God' on their side.

Eric Cantona's record in English football is nothing short of incredible. Apart from the season in which he kung-fu kicked himself (and United) out of contention, 'Dieu' – as he's more correctly known – has won the league in every English campaign in which he's taken part.

Whether at Elland Road or Old Trafford, the fantastique Frenchman has proved the undisputed architect of footballing success. It seems remarkable now, that just twelve months ago, it looked as if Cantona's love affair with English football was on the rocks. Banned for his Selhurt Park assault, chased by Inter Milan and, he felt, persecuted by the FA, the lure of the lire and lazy afternoons on the shore of Lake Como with Paul Ince beckoned.

The United fans, who were calling for Alex Ferguson's head at the start of the season, should hang their heads in shame, for when their manager persuaded Cantona to stay he might just have made the biggest managerial coup of his career. How did he manage it? It was easy; he just got down on his knees and begged. Ferguson knows that without its heart, his new Man' United team would have no soul.

"He is the best player I've ever worked with," says Fergie, who sounds more like an impassioned fan than a straight-laced manager when he speaks about his beloved number 7.

What's so incredible about Cantona, is that he's been able to produce his best this season even having undergone a complete change of on-the-pitch personality. At Upton Park this season, when Julian Dicks and Andy Cole squared up for a snarling match, the Frenchman went flying into the melée. Not to join the fracas as Cantona of old might have done, but to split it all up with a Gallic smile and a shrug of the shoulders.

The fire in Cantona's belly still rages, but he's learned not to control it, but to channel it into his football. As the man himself once said: "When you are confident you find freedom; from freedom of expression comes genius, euphoria and fire." And as every Premiership defender knows, if you play with fire you're likely to get burnt.

Eric CANTONA

Age 25

Date of Birth 22.1.71

Place of Birth Stone

Nickname Stan the Man

League Games & Goals
Crystal Palace 20 [1]
Southend 30 [15]
Nottingham Forest 64 [40]
Liverpool 31 [14]

Transfers
Wolves to Stafford Rangers [no fee recorded]
Stafford to Palace [£100,000]
Palace to Southend [£100,000]
Southend to Nott'm Forest [£2m]
Nott'm Forest to Liverpool [£8.5m]

Position/Role
A lethal striking cog in the Red machine

Word most often used to describe him
Stan-tastic

Word never used to describe him
Unassuming

> " I want to be respected for being a footballer."
>
> Stan Collymore

'm in a hotel bar in Finnish Lapland, way north of the Arctic Circle, and this guy taps me on the shoulder. He's wearing weird reindeer shoes and a hand woven multicoloured smock. "You are English?" he asks. "Who do you support?" "Newcastle," I reply. "Peter Beardsley is an old man," he says. "You'll never walk alone. Liverpool are the best. Stan the Man. Stan the Man. He is poison. You'll never walk alone."

Stan Collymore, it seems, has finally made it big. It seemed touch and go last season when he couldn't get past old man Rush and into the Liverpool team, and indeed he stated in the hallowed *FourFourTwo* magazine that he was thinking about giving up football. He vented his anger on Liverpool for signing him without knowing how he'd fit into their system, and on Roy Evans for leaving him out. In fact you name it, he wasn't happy about it.

But that's Stan for you. He's as outspoken off the pitch as he's outrageous on it, and if he felt that he deserved a place in the team, why shouldn't he make it clear to the world?

And it turns out he was right, in the end. Stan had to adapt to the Liverpool way, had to become part of a team, had to learn things the hard way, under the scrutiny of the press and a million Liverpool-haters dying for him to be a multi-million pound flop. But he did it. And now he forms part of the most lethal striking partnership in the Premiership. You don't get many duos much deadlier than Collymore and Fowler.

At Forest, Collymore ploughed a lone furrow down the middle, scoring many of his goals on the break. At Liverpool he hasn't lost any of his speed. But he's added a lot to his game, namely the ability to pop up in space, receive the ball, and give it to another player, run into space again, receive the ball again and, like as not score or set up another goal.

Nowadays it's unthinkable that Stan Collymore, red boots 'n all, might not make the Liverpool team. And he's just dying to pull on that old three-lioned shirt for England again. Stan the Man is already a bit of a household name, it seems, in Finnish Lapland. Chances are they'll be talking about him in Outer Mongolia by the time the century's out.

Stan COLLYMORE

Age 27

Date of Birth 22.4.69

Place of Birth Leicester

League Games & Goals
Cambridge Utd 156 [52]
Manchester Utd 12 [2]
Coventry City 65 [27]

Honours
1990/9 Division 3 title
[Cambridge Utd]

Transfers
Norwich to Cambridge Utd
(free)
Cambridge Utd to Manchester
Utd [£1m]
Manchester Utd to Coventry
[£2.1m]

Did you know?
Dion Dublin played centre
back for Norwich City reserves
before transferring to
Cambridge Utd

Position/Role
Grinning down to everyone else

Word most often used to describe him
Awesome

Word never used to describe him
Stocky

> "My first love has
> always been football
> and that's all I've ever
> wanted to do."
>
> Dion Dublin

ion Dublin, what a nice guy. Too nice, though, according to his manager Ron Atkinson who wants to see a little less smiling and a lot more snarling from his skipper.

"Dion's a great player with a nice disposition, but maybe that's something that's got to change if he's to make an even bigger impact on the game", says Atkinson. "If you look at most top strikers you'll see fire in their eyes, and I'd like to see a little more of that from Dion, a little more aggression."

It's not that Atkinson is displeased with the big striker, it's just that having worked with the former Cambridge and Manchester United hit-man first hand, he feels he can get even better. "He's obviously benefited from playing alongside the likes of Hughes and Cantona at United," continues Atkinson, "but I believe he can keep on improving."

A £1 million buy from Cambridge in August 1992, a few eyebrows were raised when Phil Neal gambled nearly twice that amount, one broken leg, just 12 league outings and two goals later. Dublin responded with 10 goals in 13 games (including a debut strike at QPR and an audacious overhead kick at Everton), plenty of talking on the pitch and a desire to win often masked by that big wide grin that Atkinson wants to see less of.

And although there wasn't much to smile about at Highfield Road last season, if there's one man who kept Coventry in the top flight it was big Dion. Leading from the front, never afraid to put his head in where it hurts, Dublin's vital goals were, er, vital. And when it came to backs-to-the-wall defending and half of Coventry's back-line was on the treatment table, Dublin even found himself playing as a make-shift centre-half.

When the defence is fit, however, Dublin is the focus of Atkinson's Coventry side and his aerial ability is recognised as just one, albeit major, facet of his game. If Atkinson can hold on to him – Dublin has been quoted as saying he wants to move to a club capable of putting some silverware on his mantelpiece – then maybe this season won't be quite as traumatic as the last.

Dion DUBLIN

Age 29

Date of Birth 18.12.66

Place of Birth London

League Games & Goals
QPR 163 [70]
Newcastle 37 [24]

Honours
PFA Player of the Year 1995/96

Transfers
Hayes to QPR [£15,000]
Besiktas, Turkey [loan]
QPR to Newcastle
[£6m]

Position/Role
Muscling in on any sniff of
goalmouth action

Word most often used to describe him
Monstrous

Word never used to describe him
Lightweight

> ## "I played football because I enjoyed it. I didn't think I'd become a pro."
> ### Les Ferdinand

When Les Ferdinand made the England starting line up against Bulgaria in March, the odd fickle eyebrow was raised as the Newcastle striker seemed to be off-form for his club. But Ferdinand took just six minutes to remind everyone just how good he was. Teddy Sheringham saw the centre forward charging into the box and flicked a first-time ball into his path. The pass was brilliant, but Ferdi still had plenty to do. He brushed aside a pesky fly challenge from Ivanov and chested the ball down without breaking stride, before slotting it under the advancing keeper Mihailov.

The goal was typical of the man Kevin Keegan signed at the start of the season, and was one of the 29 reasons that he was voted PFA player of the year by his colleagues. He's as strong as a tank, but to call him one would be to ignore his huge aerial presence, and his shrewd ability to play one-touch football. Ferdinand has it all: if the MOD could find an x-ray of his body they'd have the blueprint for a weapon that could keep the country rich in arms-deal money for years.

"If you've got a monster, you've got to feed it," said Kevin Keegan in August, salivating in anticipation of what the big Newcastle number 9 was going to do to Premiership defences over the forthcoming season. And, with Ferdinand exploding into form from the off, Keegan's appetite wasn't disappointed. In the autumn it wasn't a question of whether the Londoner was going to score, it was how many. If he'd carried on in that vein of form, Newcastle would have wrapped up the title by March.

As it was, the goals dried up. One problem, as Ferdinand publically stated after his England goal, was that the absence of Gillespie and the inclusion of Asprilla meant that Newcastle lost the 4-2-4 shape that had torn apart Premiership defences from the off, and created so many chances for the centre-forward.

Monsters, however, don't lose their appetite for long, and next year surely Keegan will have readjusted Newcastle's tactical formation to suit their major asset again. Goalkeepers beware.

Les FERDINAND

Age 24

Date of Birth 27.12.71

Place of Birth Stirling

League Games & Goals
Dundee United 77 [28]
Rangers 10 [1]
Everton 41 [10]

Duncan Ferguson's 1995/96 season
Interrupted by a spell at her Majesty's pleasure and a series of niggling injuries, big Dunc only managed 18 appearances and a measly five goals for the Toffees

Honours
FA Cup 1995

Did you know?
Ferguson scored on his debut for Scotland against Germany with an outrageous overhead kick

Position/Role
Headbutting the ball into the back of the net

Word most often used to describe him
Giant

Word never used to describe him
Gentle

> "He's the most frightening player I've seen in the Premiership for a long time."
>
> Duncan McKenzie.

uncan Ferguson is the best Everton striker since Alex Young. He's good-looking, articulate, looks after his mum, loves animals (especially pigeons) and does a lot of work for charity. OK call me chicken, but would you say anything against the man they call 'Duncan Disorderly' and whose assaults, shall we say, haven't always been directed towards the opposition's goal? When Ferguson turned up on loan at Goodison Park a couple of seasons ago with a hard man reputation and a string of suspended sentences and bans, no one knew quite what to expect. When he scored in the 2-0 victory over Liverpool in one of his first games for Everton, no one on the blue side of Merseyside cared. And when it later turned out he'd spent the night before out on the town – including getting arrested for drink driving – his cult status was secured.

"Big Fergie likes a few pints, loves to stay out late and chase the birds, and give a bit of lip in training," observed legendary Scottish striker, drinker and womaniser Jim Baxter. "In my book he's got all the perfect ingredients for a great footballer."

Whether he takes up Baxter's advice on how to structure his training schedule or not, after a season rudely interrupted by a quick stretch at her Majesty's pleasure, this time around Big Dunc can finally put his off the pitch problems behind him and concentrate of terrifying the life out of defenders – legally.

"He's the most frightening player I've seen in the Premiership for a long time," said ex-Everton midfielder Duncan MacKenzie. And let's face it, you have to feel sorry for the ball, let alone Ferguson's marker, when the big Scotsman thunders in for one of his trademark headers. But don't think that's all there is to his game, oh no. Give him an inch of room in or just outside the box and you're liable to pay the penalty.

But what does Ferguson himself think of his hard-man image? Is it all a myth? Underneath that rock solid shell is there a soft, fluffy centre? Er, well we were going to ask Ferguson for his thoughts, but apparently he doesn't like speaking to the media and, frankly, we were too scared to ask!

Duncan FERGUSON

Age 29

Date of Birth 3.2.67

Place of Birth Kenilworth

League Games & Goals
Wolves 63
Southampton 192
Swindon 7 (loan)
Blackburn 105

Honours
FA Premiership 1994/95

Transfers
Wolves to Southampton
[£70,000]
Swindon [loan]
Southampton to Blackburn
[£2.4m]

Position/Role
Standing in the Blackburn goal, wishing he could go back in time

Word most often used to describe him
Big-hearted

Word never used to describe him
Improved

> "He's got agility, he's got good hands, and he's brave."
>
> Pat Jennings

he look on Tim Flowers' face was priceless during Blackburn's February home defeat against Liverpool last season. Stan 'The Man' Collymore had just fluffed a daisy cutter that was rolling rather than careering towards the Rovers keeper. The ball hit a divot and spun into the air and over Flowers' shoulder to end up nestling in the net. Flowers followed the ball over his shoulder with his eyes, looking absolutely aghast. Then he looked down at the divot with an expression of sheer disgust mixed with utter disbelief.

The goal was a freak, and Flowers can't really be blamed, but in a way it summed up a frustrating season for the man who a year ago looked likely to be England's keeper for the next decade or so. The season started badly for Flowers, when Blackburn opened their Champions League campaign with a disastrous home defeat by Spartak Moscow, largely due to a blunder by the Midlander, who completely misjudged a through-ball, allowing Spartak to score the only goal of the game. To make matters worse, David Seaman hijacked the England keeper's jersey and refused to give it back.

Life is hard for keepers, their slapstick errors always spring to mind before their brilliant saves. And not many people remember the full stretch save he made from Peter Beardsley last season that, in effect, gave Blackburn two points that proved vital to their championship win. Or a host of other stops, not least the one from a close range Beresford shot in the same game, that Flowers got a hand to, despite it having already passed under his body.

"He's got all it takes to make a world class goalkeeper," says Pat Jennings, record cap holder for Northern Ireland, former Spurs and Arsenal goalie and currently goalkeeping trainer at Tottenham: a man who knows a thing or two about life between the sticks. "He's got agility, he's got good hands, he's got anticipation, he's brave and he reads the game well."

Last season he made far too many mistakes to be put in the world class category, but last season, surely, was an aberration. Next season, wise money will be on Tim Flowers being remembered for all the right reasons.

Tim FLOWERS

Age 21

Date of Birth 9.4.75

Place of Birth
Liverpool

League Games & Goals
Liverpool 108 [64]

Robbie Fowler's 1995/96 season
An astonishing 28 league goals in 38 games, putting him second only to Shearer in the goalscoring chart. Made his England debut v Bulgaria.

Honours
Coca Cola Cup 1995

Did you know?
Robbie Fowler had a bust-up with Neil 'Razor' Ruddock last season, which ended with the pair coming to blows. Apparently Fowler had cut up Ruddock's best shoes

Position/Role
Scoring goals and grinning cheekily

Word most often used to describe him
Deadly

Word never used to describe him
Wasteful

> "He could be the greatest they've ever had at Liverpool."
>
> Graeme Souness

What are Robbie Fowler's strengths? OK it's a stupid question, but Ronnie Moran's reply isn't. "He scores goals," says the Liverpool coach. Scoring goals is what Robbie Fowler does. Last season he scored an incredible 28 in 38 games. He scored headers and volleys, tap-ins and long range piledrivers. He won the PFA Young Player of the Year Award for the second year in succession, he played for England and even survived a right hook from Razor Ruddock. What a year!

Liverpool legend Graeme Souness, the man who gave Fowler his debut when he was Anfield boss, reckons the 22-year-old hit-man is one in a million. "He could be the greatest they've ever had at Liverpool," says Souness. "Robbie has more natural ability than Ian Rush. Rushie had an incredible ability to sniff out a chance. Fowler has got that, too, but also has the ability to take the ball outside the box and do something great."

The way Robbie Fowler played last season, who'd be a goalkeeper? Mark Bosnich, who conceded four to the Reds' number 23 last season, is just glad he doesn't have to face him every week and rates him ahead of Alan Shearer as the goalkeepers union's most feared opponent.

"He often shoots early, doesn't mind where he shoots from and seems to get late fade on his shots, like a golfer," says Bosnich. "But the main reason he scores so many is less complicated. He usually gets 10 out of 10 shots on target, and with nine out of 10 he'll hit the corners. His accuracy is quite amazing."

The only thing that can stop Fowler reaching the very top would seem to be his attitude, and, unfortunately for Bosnich and his goalkeeping compadres, there doesn't seem to be too much to worry about there either.

"You've got to have a certain arrogance to be a good player, but Robbie's no big-head," says Ronnie Moran. "There's so much going on in the heads of these young players, especially if they become superstars, and some can handle it and some can't. Robbie can."

Robbie FOWLER

Age 22

Date of Birth 29.11.73

Place of Birth Cardiff

Nickname Er, Giggsy

Appearances and goals
Manchester United 177 [37]

Ryan Giggs' 1995/96 season
A back-to-his-best 11 goals in 33 league games including the very last one of the campaign, a 30-yarder at Middlesbrough

Honours
Rumbelows Cup 1992
Premiership 1992/93, 1993/94 and 1995/96
FA Cup 1994 and 1996

Position/Role
Breaking the hearts of young girls and defenders alike with his lethal runs

Word most often used to describe him
Genius

Word never used to describe him
Disappointing

> "He makes you believe there is a football God after all."
>
> Ron Atkinson

When a tricky new winger starts catching the eye in the Manchester United youth team nowadays they don't say, "Wow, he could be the new George Best," they say, "Wow, he could be the new Ryan Giggs." And as Best himself says: "One day they might even say I was another Ryan Giggs!"

At just 22 years of age, Ryan Giggs is already an Old Trafford legend. And as a veteran of five seasons in United's first team, he's now the wise old man in Fergie's team of fledglings.

Despite the best attempts of the tabloids, he's proved he has what it takes in the brain department to keep his life in order, as well as what he has in his feet to leave opposition defences in tatters. He's overcome the worst injury problems of his career and come back better than ever. At the end of last season his form was awesome. He still has the pace and trickery that once prompted a £10 million bid from AC Milan (whose coach Fabio Capello said: "Like George Best, he has that special fantasia about him") but he's added the maturity and consistency that turn a good player into a great one.

Even when he was suffering from hamstring problems and a knee injury last season, the footballing world continued to cast admiring glances in the Welsh international's direction.

So what's he worth then: £10 million, £12 million, £14 million? The papers are full of the figures AC Milan and Barcelona are prepared to pay for him. But Giggs, the son of a Welsh rugby league player, says he's "going nowhere".

And why should he? He's playing in just about the best team in the land, he's just signed a multi-million pound boot deal with Reebok and his beautiful girlfriend has just moved into his new £750,000 mansion. It's not as if there's anything missing in his life. Still, no doubt they'll keep trying.

"I'd break the bank to buy Ryan Giggs tomorrow if I could," says Ron Atkinson. "He makes you believe there is a football God after all."

Ryan GIGGS

Age 21

Date of Birth 18.2.1975

Place of Birth
Lame, Northern Ireland

League Games & Goals by club
Wigan 8 [4]
Manchester United 8 [1]
Newcastle United 45 [5]

Keith Gillespie's 95/96 season
Played 28 times for
Newcastle and scored three
goals. He created a lot more!

Transfers
Man Utd to Wigan (loan)
Man Utd to Newcastle (part of
Andy Cole tranfer, valued at
£1m)

Did you know?
Keith Gillespie's first ever
league goal was for Man Utd
in 1994… against Newcastle

Position/Role
Tearing defences apart or
tearing his hair out on the
bench

Word most often used to describe him
Lightning

Word never used to describe him
Tino

"It is an advantage for me to have a winger in the team."

Les Ferdinand

austino Asprilla arrived in Newcastle amidst a flurry of media hype and, almost immediately, Newcastle's title hopes started to wane. Not because the Colombian international wasn't any good; not at all, English fans had never seen anything like his rubbery-legged ball mastery, and neither had defenders. But perhaps because, almost unnoticed, the arrival of the South American meant that a 20-year-old winger from Larne in Northern Ireland lost his place in the team. United lost their shape – and the Premiership.

Gillespie's exit from the team – which came just after he'd recovered from injury – coincided with a bout of rustiness from Newcastle's goal machine Les Ferdinand. But the coincidence wasn't casual. "If you have seen the way I play you will know it is an advantage for me to have a winger in the team," said Ferdinand from England's training camp before the Bulgaria game last season. The tabloids went barmy, branding the Asprilla-Gillespie swap as a 'Kev Boob', positively revelling in the chance to dig their talons into the hitherto untouchable manager. They had a point though, because with Ginola down one wing and Gillespie down the other, United were a deadly attacking force. To put it simply, Gillespie's sheer pace and ability to get crosses in from the right made more chances than Asprilla's more subtle, but less direct, trickery.

Gillespie was to hit the headlines himself last season, but at the wrong end of the paper. *The Sun* broke the story that he'd blown rather a lot of dosh in a mad gambling spree. Gillespie ended up looking the way full backs usually look when he leaves them in his wake: rather silly.

But the Northern Ireland international, who was the 'million pound makeweight' in the deal that unloaded Andy Cole on to Manchester United, will now have to prove that he has the maturity and level-headedness to take the whole affair in his considerable stride and get back to doing what he does best – helping Newcastle United to win. By the end of last season, he was back in the team and back terrorising defences, albeit too late for the Toon Army. Luckily for them, his best is surely yet to come.

Keith GILLESPIE

Age 29

Date of Birth 25.1.67

Place of Birth Gassin [France]

League Games & Goals
Toulon 81 [4]
Racing Paris 61 [8]
Brest 50 [10]
Paris St. Germain 115 [32]
Newcastle United 34 (5)

Honours
French League winner, twice
French Cup winner and French
League Cup winner [all with
Paris St Germain]

Position/Role
Treating right-backs to a view
of his backside most girls
would kill for

**Word most often used to describe
him**
Fantastique

Word never used to describe him
Ugly

> "I read Batman and Superman when I was a child. They are super-heroes. Not a footballer, which is a job." David Ginola

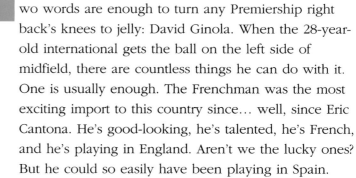

Two words are enough to turn any Premiership right back's knees to jelly: David Ginola. When the 28-year-old international gets the ball on the left side of midfield, there are countless things he can do with it. One is usually enough. The Frenchman was the most exciting import to this country since… well, since Eric Cantona. He's good-looking, he's talented, he's French, and he's playing in England. Aren't we the lucky ones?

But he could so easily have been playing in Spain. Barcelona were favourites amongst a host of clubs looking to buy Ginola but asked him to wait whilst the futures of Stoichkov and Hagi were sorted out. With Newcastle and Arsenal pounding on his door, he told them where to go with their waiting. Newcastle offered him wages Arsenal couldn't afford, and now he's the toast of the Toon, the 'frog (prince) on the Tyne'.

Ginola couldn't wait to leave Paris St. Germain, where (nicknamed El Magnifico) he had played since 1991, winning the French Championship, the French Cup (twice), the French League Cup, and helped steer the side to three European competition semi-finals. Why? Because he didn't get on with the manager, Luis Fernandez, who wanted to change the way he played, and wouldn't let him play golf. Kevin Keegan is much more open to his needs. "He can play golf every day if he likes as long as he plays football like that," says the Magpies' manager after one full-back roasting performance last season.

Ginola immediately clicked with his boss, and fitted neatly into Newcastle's attack-at-all-costs style, teaching those around him a thing or two about how to play, but picking up the odd tip, too. "English football is very different. I want to learn the fighting spirit of the English game," he said.

Ginola, though, found it tough to get goals last season, but Keegan bought him to feed Ferdinand, and the Frenchman was directly responsible for many of the striker's early-season glut of goals. The mesmerising way in which he went about getting the ball across the box, have made him the most popular player on Tyneside since his boss was wearing black and white stripes.

David GINOLA

Age 22

Date of Birth 3.8.74

Place of Birth
Sunderland

League Games & Goals
111 [8]

Michael Gray's 1995/96 season
A cracker, starring in every one of Sunderland's 46 league games and hitting five goals

Honours
Division One Title 1995/96

Did you know?
Michael Gray was a trainee at Man Utd and played alongside Gary Neville, Nicky Butt and David Beckham

Position/Role
Trying to beat defenders without getting his hair in his eyes

Word most often used to describe him
Colourful

Word never used to describe him
Grey

"Michael has been quite outstanding for us, but I know there's a lot more to come from the lad."

Peter Reid

t's likely to be a tough battle for survival in the Premiership this season for Sunderland. But if the Rokermen do survive – or even thrive – you can bet Michael Gray will have had plenty to do with it.

Sunderland born and bred, Gray has stood out like a beacon in the Endsleigh League this season and not just because of his long, blond locks. A speedy, skilful, left-sided attacker, it can't be long before people start making the Ryan Giggs comparisons. But, ironically, Giggs is one reason why Gray ended up at Roker Park.

A few years ago Gray was on Manchester United's books, playing alongside Fergie fledglings such as Gary Neville, Nicky Butt and David Beckham. "But I always knew that with Ryan Giggs at the club I was never going to get a look in at United," he explains, and so when Sunderland came in for him in 1992 he jumped at the chance of first team football at his hometown club.

For the first three or four seasons, like the fortunes of the club itself, life at Sunderland was full of ups and downs for Gray. One week he'd be inspired, the next anonymous, and it took the arrival of the inspirational Peter Reid as manager to change all that.

"When the boss arrived he just told me to run at players, to make life difficult for them," he explains. "That's what I enjoy doing and that's what I'll continue to do."

And the Sunderland supremo himself is full of praise for his young star. They may sing "Cheer up Peter Reid" at Roker Park, but if Reid had 11 Michael Grays to put in his team they'd be getting sick of him sporting a grin wider than the Wear all day long. "Michael has been quite outstanding for us," says Reid, although, as if with the words of the song terrace anthem ringing in his head, he adds: "But I know there's a lot more to come from the lad."

It hasn't all been sweetness and light, though. Last season the pair had an on the pitch bust-up, but Sunderland fans will be relieved to know they've patched up their differences now. They know that if they're going to bridge the ever-widening gap between the Endsleigh league and the Premiership, they're going to need players like Michael Gray like the city of Sunderland needs top flight football.

Michael GRAY

Age 33

Date of Birth 1.9.62

Place of Birth Amsterdam

League Games & Goals
Haarlem 91 [31]
Feyenoord 85 [30]
PSV Eindhoven 68 [46]
AC Milan [Italy] 125 [38]
Sampdoria [Italy] 53 [24]
Chelsea 37 [3]

Honours
Dutch Championship
[1985, 1986, 1987 with
Feyenoord and PSV]
Italian Scudetto
1988, 1992 and 1993
European Cup 1989/90
European Championships
[Holland] 1988

Position/Role
Sweeper, cum midfield general
cum striker extraordinaire

Word most often used to describe him
Class

Word never used to describe him
Rude

"If I wanted to be an individual I would play tennis." Ruud Gullit

The knees might be a bit dodgy and one of the weapons in the Surinam-born player's vast armoury – pace – isn't what it used to be. But none of that matters really because Ruud Gullit's most powerful footballing asset is his brain, which is just as well, because now he's taken over as Chelsea coach, he's sure going to need it. When Glenn Hoddle signed the 33-year-old on a free transfer from Sampdoria last summer, he wasn't snapping up a faded has-been to notch up the Stamford Bridge crowd. Far from it. Hoddle signed a masterful tactician who knew more about the game than anyone in the country and was able to teach more than a thing or two to the players around him. He signed an on-field coach as well as a world class player, and, in turn, Gullit helped transform Chelsea from a group of workaday tryers into a side that could, on their day, beat the best in the land.

Now Gullit's role as player-coach is official, and the Chelsea fans will be expecting AC Milan-like performances from the boys in blue every week. Even if they don't get them from the likes of Paul Furlong and John Spencer, however, at least they know the Dutch master will still be out there performing his art.

As a mere player last season Gullit was a joy to watch. A remarkable reader of the game, he's a player who always has space and time. He is a defender, a midfielder and an attacker rolled into one, a man with such awe-inspiring grace and class that he influences the kids who see him on TV and then go for a kickaround in the park as much as the Chelsea players.

The irony is that he might have been playing in England as a teenager. When he was strutting his stuff for Haarlem in Holland in 1980, two men went a-scouting to look at him: Don Howe, then of Arsenal, and Ipswich's Bobby Robson. Although the asking price was a mere £80,000, neither man thought him good enough to take the plunge.

How he's proved them wrong. This season, however, he has to prove himself all over again and the football world wonders how he will handle the pressure of coaching in the hurly burly of the Premiership. Chances are he'll be as calm as he is on the ball.

Ruud GULLIT

Age 27

Date of Birth 8.11.68

Place of Birth London

League Games & Goals
Watford 16 [3]
Carlisle 4 [1] loan
Port Vale 6 [2] loan
Swansea 5 [1] loan
Brentford 7 [1] loan
Brentford 110 [53]
Wimbledon 139 [53]

Transfers
Watford to Carlisle, Swansea and Brentford [loans]
Watford to Brentford [£125,000]
Brentford to Wimbledon [£720,000]

Position/Role
Trying to finish off opponents without getting too muddy

Did you know?
Dean Holdsworth's twin brother, David, plays for Watford and marked Dean out of the game when the Dons met the Hornets in the FA Cup last season

Word most often used to describe him
Smoothie

Word never used to describe him
Rugged

> "I get a buzz from scoring goals."
> Dean Holdsworth

He may have slicked back hair and facial features straight off the catwalks of Milan, but it's not Dean Holdsworth's modelling contracts that make him Top Man in the Premiership.

Holdsworth is one of those strikers who seems to amble about doing nothing for 89 minutes, then, just when you think he's not going to put a hair out of place all day, he comes alive in the box and the ball's in the back of the net.

Goalscoring is an art form, and Deano's become a bit of an old master in the Premiership after his £750,000 move from Third Division Brentford in 1992. He even owns a bronze bust of his highly sought-after features, a gift from Dons' owner Sam Hammam after his star striker hit 15 goals in his second season at Wimbledon. The following year, Hammam kissed a camel's backside when Deano hit his tally. Reports this year that he would get a brand new Ferrari when he notched up 15 goals turned out to be wishful thinking, which was probably because it was Deano himself who started the rumours.

Whether he's playing for pride or a brand new Testarossa, however, one thing's for certain: when Dean Holdsworth runs on to the pitch his mind is on one thing and one thing only. "I never go on to the pitch thinking I'm not going to score," says Holdsworth. "I always go out there to score."

Not that it's all been sweetness and light for Holdsworth over the years. After being rejected by Watford – where twin brother David still plays at centre-half – it was only when he started to find his form at Brentford that it looked like he might ever make a decent forward, let alone a pundit on Sky Sports.

These days Deano never seems to be out of the top goalscorers' chart and still dreams of an England call-up after a couple of appearances for the B team early in Venables' reign. And when he's not busy scoring goals, of course, you'll find him appearing on TV and strutting his stuff in designer labels. Nice work if you can get it. Deano gets it.

Dean HOLDSWORTH

Age 23

Date of Birth 22.2.73

Place of Birth Sao Paulo [Brazil]

Nickname
Juninho means 'little one'

League games and goals
Sao Paolo 101 [15]
Middlesbrough 21 [2]

Honours
Super Copa 1993
Recopa 1993 and 1994
World Club Championship
[v AC Milan] 1994
[all with Sao Paolo]

Transfers
Ituano to Sao Paolo (£350,000)
Sao Paolo to Middlesbrough
[£4.75m]

Position/Role
Slipping skillfully between
defenders' legs

**Word(s) most often used to
describe him**
Mighty midget

Word never used to describe him
Manly

> "He can become the best
> player in the world."
>
> Bryan Robson

**W**hen Brazilian coach Mario Zagalo first handed Juninho the famous yellow and green number 10 shirt, Brazil captain Dunga exclaimed: "What are you giving that shirt to a skinny little kid for?" By half-time the latest player to be dubbed "the new Pele" had shoved Dunga's words back down his throat with the kind of skill, vision and blistering pace now being witnessed by Premiership crowds up and down the country.

The secret of his success? He's full of beans, literally. The 5ft 5ins, 22-year-old, the current Brazilian Footballer of the Year, has had sackfuls of Brazilian beans especially shipped over to Teesside for his mum to cook up for him. (In fact, he's brought his whole family with him to 'Boro).

His manager Bryan Robson probably doesn't care what he eats, just as long as he keeps pulling on that red shirt. The 'Boro boss had been tracking him at his old club Sao Paulo for a year (after a South American 'Boro fan alerted him to the young star), but when he saw him tear England, Sweden and Japan apart in the Umbro Cup last summer he declared, "I must have him."

After a wild goose chase across Brazil, and to the surprise of the people of Brazil, of Teesside and just about everyone else in the entire footballing world, Robson signed his man. When the signing was announced, Middlesbrough went mad. Sales of 'Boro season tickets rocketed from 20,000 to 27,000, Umbro shipped its entire stock of 2000 Brazil shirts to the club shop and the whole lot were sold out within days. They even started selling Juninho burgers outside the Cellnet Riverside Stadium (served with a spicy salsa sauce of course).

Unfortunately the arrival of Juninho (Brazilian for 'little one'), coincided with a run of form which made previously high-flying Middlesbrough look more like Middle Yallop reserves. While Juninho dazzled and danced his way through the second half of the season, the team slouched its way down the table.

Whatever the reasons for the side's decline, 'Boro boss Bryan Robson will be expecting more from a team which has such talent at its heart. As Captain Marvel himself says: "Juninho can become the best player in the world." Now all he needs is another ten players to match.

JUNINHO

Age 27

Date of Birth 23.1.69

Place of Birth
Kirovograd [Ukraine]

Nickname Kan Kan

League Games & Goals
Manchester United 123 [28]
Everton 32 [16]

Andrei Kanchelskis's 1995/96 season
After his on-off transfer from United, Kanchelskis was electric for Everton. His best moment came when he scored four goals in the 5-2 win over Sheffield Wednesday

Honours
1992/93 and 1993/94 Premiership
1994 FA Cup [with Man Utd]

Did you know?
Before moving to Man Utd in 1991, Kanchelskis played for Russian team Shakhytor Denezts

Position/Role
Tearing at great speed [between great clubs]

Word[s] most often used to describe him
Fast mover

Word never used to describe him
Loyal

> "His speed and control are amazing."
>
> Joe Royle

fter a transfer saga that threatened to drag on so long he was into his third reading of *War and Peace*, Andrei Kanchelskis's on-off move to Everton was suddenly 'on' and he was cleared to play. And the opponents in his first game for the Toffees was... Manchester United! With feelings running high between the clubs, especially after Kanchelskis declared he no longer wanted to play for United, they practically exploded when Lee Sharpe sent the Russian international tumbling on the right touchline, dislocating his shoulder and condemning him to finish at least another eight chapters of Tolstoy's classic while he recovered.

Sharpe pleaded his innocence, and the challenge was purely accidental, but the travelling fans from Manchester greeted his departure with their biggest cheer of the day.

Kanchelskis, who in the absence of Cantona the previous season had proved United's most potent force with his electrifying pace down the right flank, had angered the Manchester club. Alex Ferguson, who denied he'd had a bust-up with the Ukraine-born star and tried in vain to persuade him to change his mind, declared he was more concerned about losing Kanchelskis than either Paul Ince or Mark Hughes. So why did the flying winger turn his back on the biggest club in the land? Well, the small matter of a few hundred grand in signing on fees might have had something to do with it, although he was hardly playing for peanuts at Old Trafford.

Whatever the reasons, United's loss was Everton's gain and Kanchelskis was soon to be found tearing past defenders, cutting in and going for goal in the blue shirt like he always had in a red one. His penchant for racing into the box and scoring from all sorts of ludicrous angles, had Joe Royle drooling and, for the first time in several years, Everton were fighting for a place in Europe and not battling against the dreaded drop.

"He's an excellent player," says Everton boss Joe Royle. "His speed and control are amazing. I was delighted to get him."

Which, funnily enough, is exactly what Lee Sharpe said after that match at Goodison. Allegedly.

Andrei KANCHELSKIS

Age 26

Date of Birth 10.8.71

Place of Birth Cork

Nickname Keano

League Games & Goals
Nottingham Forest 114 [22]
Manchester United 91 [13]

Roy Keane's 1995/96 season
Back in his favoured central midfield role, Keane played 29 of United's 38 league games and scored six goals

Honours
Premiership 1993/94 and 1995/96
FA Cup 1994 and 1996
[With Man Utd]

Position/Role
Running midfield and trying to keep his hair on

Word most often used to describe him
Hot

Word never used to describe him
Softy

"The ball's there to be won."

Roy Keane

f it hadn't been for Roy Keane, Paul Ince would probably never have been sold to Inter Milan. For as Ince flew off to a new life in Serie A, Alex Ferguson only had to glance across the training pitch to check on the progress of the man most qualified to succeed him.

Keane was tailor-made to fill Ince's boots. Like Ince though, the 26-year-old Irishman has taken a while to settle into a rhythm at Old Trafford and has sometimes taken the 'battling' qualities of his game too literally. Last season he marred a superb run of form in United's midfield with a couple of crazy Kamikaze sendings-off.

But apart from when the red mist rises (usually closely followed by the red card rising), Keane is the driving force behind United's midfield. One moment he's providing a platform for the likes of Giggs and Cantona with his hard-running, hard-tackling, never-say-die spirit, the next he's able to break forward with super skill and deadly awareness. Oh yeah, and he doesn't like losing either.

"The gaffer wouldn't have any of us in the team if we didn't have that spirit," says Keane. "It's all right being skilful, but you've got to have the will to win. After all, that's the whole point of the game."

If Keane can curb his temper and cut-out the crazy flashpoints, then, by the end of this season, the United fans might have forgotten Paul Ince ever existed. He's grown his hair and, to sighs of relief around the footballing world, abandoned the aggressive aerodynamic pudding bowl look. Now he has to trim his temperament to match.

The irony is, that off the pitch, the lad from Cork is one of the mildest mannered players in the whole United squad. And over the years he's already calmed down plenty. Nowadays, he nips down his local every now and again instead of spending every night out on the town with the boys.

There'll be plenty hoping Roy Keane will shoot himself in the foot again a few times this coming season, but after what they saw last season they won't be banking on it.

Roy KEANE

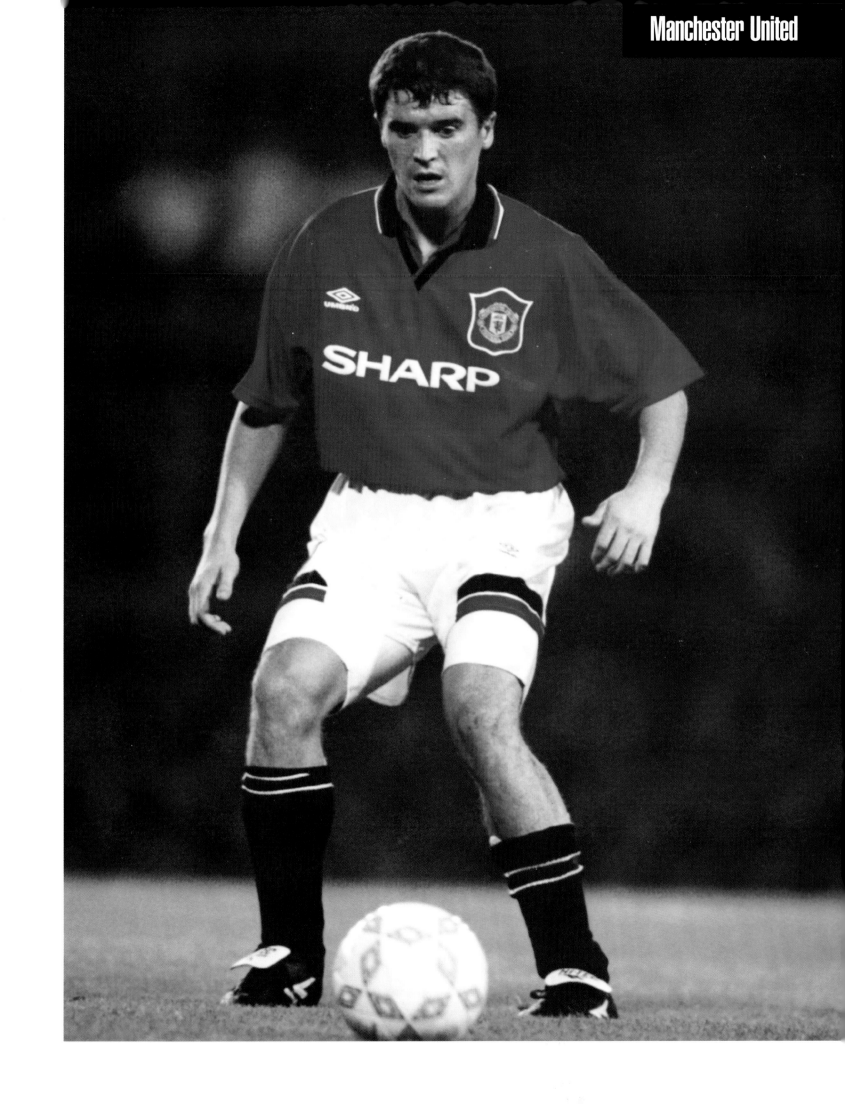

Age 28

Date of Birth 17.10.68

Place of Birth Jersey

Nickname
Rag [after the number plate on his old car]

League Games & Goals
Chelsea 90 [8]
Blackburn 103 [4]

Graeme Le Saux's 1995/96 season
Played 14 games for Blackburn and scored one goal until injury ruined his season, as well as his Euro 96 dream

Honours
Premiership winner 1994/95

Did you know?
Before being injured Graeme had played in every England game under Terry Venables.

Position/Role
Thrusting down the left with his hair tufting up in the wind

Word most often used to describe him
Unlucky

Word[s] never used to describe him
Right-sided

> "I would be a liar if I said football was the most important thing in my life."
>
> Graeme Le Saux

It was quite a season for Graeme 'Tintin' Le Saux, one straight out of the Hammer House of Horror. What a contrast from the previous one when his name was just about the first on Terry Venables' England team-sheet, when he won the Premiership title with Blackburn, and then rounded things off nicely with a Brazilian-style goal against the Brazilians themselves in the Umbro Cup.

It was bad enough getting into a fight with David Batty in freezing cold Moscow during Blackburn's ill-starred Champions League campaign. But that was chicken feed compared to the horrific ankle injury he suffered against Middlesbrough that left him with a shattered ankle and his European Championship dreams in tatters.

Since then, Le Saux has been sorely missed by club and country alike. England had been screaming for a talented left-sided player for years and he really fits the bill, able to operate as a traditional full back or a marauding wing-back.

That goal against Brazil was ample proof of Le Saux's potency as an attacking force. The ball was headed clear from a Pearce corner and bounced awkwardly in front of Le Saux. He calmly chested it down and thwacked a dipper over keeper Zetti to put England in the lead against the World Champions. "That was a really good way to finish a really good season," he said later. "It's the sort of thing you can't imagine happening to you. It just came right for me and flew into the top corner."

Poor Le Saux, the higher you peak the harder you fall, and the Blackburn physio's bench must seem a long way from a packed Wembley in June. Still, the 28-year-old is a great reader (and we're talking more Brett Easton Ellis than Jeffrey Archer) so he should have been able to while away the interminable hours a little.

Le Saux will obviously be affected by his long lay-off, and it will be a real test of character to see if he can play his way back into the England team. One thing's for sure: he'll be looking to the future with more appetite than he's looking back on the immediate past. But 1995/6 is a season he'll try to forget as quickly as he usually scurries up the left wing.

Graeme LE SAUX

Age 27

Date of Birth 14.10.68

Place of Birth Guernsey

Nickname God

League Games & Goals
   Southampton 326 [126]

Matt Le Tissier's 1995/96 season
   A complete nightmare by his standards. He played in 34 league games for the Saints but could only muster 7 goals even though he takes the penalties!

Position/Role
   Marauding genius who looks like he's pulling a strop... even when he's just scored from 45 yards

Word most often used to describe him
   Enigma

Word[s] never used to describe him
   England regular

> "He's a star horse in a stable full of handicappers."
>
> Alan Ball

uddenly nobody's begging for Matt Le Tissier to be put in the England team any more. After the extraordinary performances he made in the previous two years at Southampton, the attacking midfielder has had a bit of a nightmare of it this time round. Blame it on the hype, blame it on Venables, blame it on yourself for screaming his praises to the treetops.

"There is no doubt that his England rejection hit him hardest of all," says his manager Dave Merrington. "Matt's confidence has been shot this season. It has affected him badly. Now he will be the first to admit he does not deserve to play for his country."

It's a far cry from last time round when he won, for the second time, the Goal of the Season award for the BBC and a place in every punter's England XI.

"Only Matt Le Tissier can do that..." enthused Motty at the time, as the Southampton lynchpin turned to celebrate a dipping 40 yarder that caught Blackburn keeper Tim Flowers inches out of position, but yards away from getting a hand to the ball "...because only he would have thought of it!"

Funny old game, football, and without the cocky confidence that gave Le Tissier the ideas, he hasn't been able to reproduce the magic. The magic is still in there somehere, though.

"He's one of very few players I've seen with all-round ability," drools Manchester City manager Alan Ball about his former charge. "He can play it long, he can play it short, he's superbly precise in his passing, he's a magnificent manipulator and he can make and score goals. In short, he's a one-off."

The Channel Islander first caught the eye in a Southampton youth team attack which also included Rodney Wallace and Alan Shearer. "Wallace had the pace, Shearer had the strength, and Le Tissier had the natural ability. And still has," says Chris Nicholl, Saints manager at the time.

Last year he was too good to get into the England team, this year he's not good enough. But ability has a crafty knack of shining through, and Le Tissier will be back. God help goalkeepers.

Matt LE TISSIER

Age 26

Date of Birth 17.8.70

Place of Birth Norway

**League Games & Goals
[where known]**
Clausenegen [Norway]
Molde [Norway]
Rosenborg [Norway]
Wimbledon 48 [8]

Leonhardsen's 1995/96 season
Played in 28 of Wimbledon's
Premiership matches, netting
four goals. Also earned himself
the Player of the Season award
at Selhurst Park

Norway appearances
Full 48
U21 14
U19 5
U18 4
Youth 30

Transfers
Molde to Rosenborg [£90,000]
Rosenborg to Wimbledon
[£700,000]

Position/Role
Mixing graft with craft
for 90 minutes

**Word most often used to describe
him**
Energetic

Word never used to describe him
Drunk

> "I aim to go as far as
> I can in football."
>
> Oyvind Leonhardsen

Think of Norwegian football and what springs to mind? A mad commentator poking fun at Winston Churchill and Maggie Thatcher and a bunch of boring long-ballers. Oyvind Leonhardsen is doing his best to change all that. Despite plying his trade last season in the hurly burly of Wimbledon's midfield, the 25-year-old Norwegian international has emerged as one of the craftiest, classiest middle of the park players in the Premiership. He's not the archetypal Crazy Gang player at all. He doesn't even drink.

"It's not that I don't like beer," he says. "But I couldn't drink like they do. Not during the season anyway." Even without an insatiable lust for lager, Leonhardsen settled straight into the Dons' side when he arrived on loan from Norwegian champions Rosenborg in October 1995. The rumours that he now speaks better English than Joe Kinnear, Sam Hammam and Vinnie Jones put together aren't far from the truth, and his inspired performances on the pitch led to Kevin Keegan asking Joe Kinnear to name his price if he ever wanted to sell his hard running star.

It didn't take Leonhardsen long to make an impact on English football – about 90 minutes in fact. On-loan and out to impress, he scored the last-minute winner in his first match, a 4-3 thriller against Aston Villa, which not only landed him a contract with the Dons but dumped Villa boss Ron Atkinson out of a job. "That was a great moment and it helped me a lot," he says, though he neglects to share his thoughts on the demise of one of English football's great figures.

Oyvind has more than 40 caps for his country, making his debut, aged 19, a few months after playing in the World Youth Cup in 1989. Back home in Norway he's a recognised everywhere he goes. With the Scandinavian penchant for English football (the BBC beams its Match of the Day fixtures live to Norway every Saturday), the Norwegian media follow his every move as they do all foreign imports. For the last year and a half, like Premiership crowds up and down the country, they've been enjoying what they've been seeing.

Oyvind LEONHARDSEN

Age 31

Date of Birth 25.12.64

Place of Birth Motherwell

League games and goals
Motherwell 59 [6]
Leicester 201 [47]
Leeds 206 [33]

Honours
First Division Championship
1991/92

Transfers
Motherwell to Leicester
[£125,000]
Leicester to Leeds [£1m]

Position/Role
Singlehandedly making
Leeds look like a good
team

Word most often used to describe him
Consistent

Word never used to describe him
Expendable

> "The players I most modelled myself on were Ray Wilkins and Glenn Hoddle."
>
> Gary McAllister

ort Vale fans don't like Gary McAllister very much. It's the last minute of their FA Cup replay against Leeds and they're drawing 1-1 with the illustrious Yorkshiremen. Not a good time to give away a free kick outside the box with the canny Scots midfielder around. McAllister twists the ball round the wall and into the top right-hand corner of the net, to put Leeds into the glam new BBC draw.

It was a pretty dreadful season for Leeds one way or another, especially as it promised so well in the heady days of autumn with success coming easy at home and on the continent, and Tony Yeboah on fire. But one man has been consistent throughout the year. McAllister, unlike Leeds, doesn't run hot and cold, and their skipper has strung another characteristically consistent set of performances together, as well as masterminding Scotland's qualification into the Euro 96 finals.

McAllister's midfield style – simple ball, simple ball, outrageous spot-on 50 yard pass – is reminiscent of Glenn Hoddle, so it's no surprise the Chelsea manager was an early role model for Gary. "The players I most modelled myself on were Ray Wilkins and particularly Glenn Hoddle," he says. "I admired Hoddle's technique, his touch, his ability to control the ball and always pick the right pass, whether it was long or short. He'd always put his head up to look at his options and I'd like to think I've learnt that lesson off him."

He also scores more than either Hoddle or Wilkins ever did, which makes him one of a rare breed: the goalscoring playmaker. It's difficult to think of a team that the soft-spoken Motherwell-born 31-year-old wouldn't grace, especially as he plays with the sort of quintadonna attitude that managers can only dream of getting from most players.

"He's a great enthusiast," says Tommy McLean, his boss when he started out for his hometown team. "He'd approach a junior match with the same vigour as he would an international."

Leeds fans will be hoping he'll be doing so for some years to come. They need him.

Gary McALLISTER

Age 24

Date of Birth 11.2.72

Place of Birth Liverpool

Nickname
Macca/Shaggy

League Games & Goals
Liverpool 180 [25]

Honours
FA Cup 1992
Coca Cola Cup 1995

Steve McManaman's 1995/96 season
Played in all but two of Liverpool's 38 league games, playing superbly but scoring a disappointing 6 goals

Did you know?
Sir Stanley Matthews once complimented Steve on his 'dribbling'

Position/Role
Trying to beat defenders before he snaps in half

Word most often used to describe him
Cheeky

Word never used to describe him
Chubby

> "Imagine him running at you every game. You'd be shi**ing yourself wouldn't you?"
>
> Robbie Fowler

When asked once what he'd like to have with him if he was marooned on a desert island, Steve McManaman replied, "Pele, so he could teach me a few things." The way the young Liverpool midfielder's played over the past couple of years, however, the world's greatest ever player might find the lessons equally rewarding. McManaman's breathtaking ability to run at and beat defenders at will, his spindly body gyrating wildly and the ball apparently glued to his left foot, inevitably smacks of the days when shorts were baggy (yes, even baggier than Blackburn's current design) and every team had two wingers. But McManaman is not really a winger. His strength is not in beating men, getting to the by-line and firing in crosses, he's at his best when he's skipping past tackles, cutting in from the by-line and going straight for goal.

Last season, handed a free role by Liverpool boss Roy Evans, McManaman was on fire. And by the time Euro 96 came around he was a regular for England and was starting to show the kind of form he showed every week at Anfield, but this time against the defenders of Bulgaria and Croatia not Bolton and Coventry.

Still only 25, McManaman – who made his debut way back in 1990 – has now played nearly 200 league games for Liverpool after being snapped up from right under the noses of the Everton scouts as an 11-year-old, ironic seeing as he was a true blue Everton fan with Bob Latchford and Duncan MacKenzie posters plastered all over his walls.

"He always had confidence, even then," recalls Liverpool assistant manager Ronnie Moran. "When you saw him coming down the corridor you'd think, 'Aye, aye, who's this then?' He walked with a swagger like he does now. But he's no bighead, he's a sensible lad who looks after himself, and that's why he's made it."

Despite some great goals for the Reds last season, if there's one area in which McManaman's game could improve, it's his shooting. But Premiership defenders will be dismayed to hear he's staying behind after training to work on his only weakness. Gulp!

Steve McMANAMAN

Age 29

Date of Birth 22.9.66

Place of Birth
Stepney

League games & goals
Tottenham 21 [1]
Cambridge 4 [0]
Doncaster 4 [0]
Portsmouth 7 [0]
Brentford 51 [0]
Ipswich 6 [0]
Swindon 58 [5]
West Ham 62 [4]

Moncur's 1995/96 season
Played 32 games for
West Ham, scoring twice

Position/Role
Creator of chances for
West Ham strikers to miss

Word most often used to describe him
Patient

Word never used to describe him
Uncultured

> ## "I like to get hold of the ball and pass it to other players."
> John Moncur

"can't say too much, the manager's on me shoulder" says West Ham midfielder John Moncur down the telephone from the club's training ground when asked what his strengths are.

"I like to get hold of the ball, I guess, and pass it to other players."

But in a nutshell, he'd summarised his role at West Ham. He was being modest of course, because he's very very good at getting hold of the ball and giving it to other players. Moncur has an astute sense of when to make and how to weigh the right pass and a penchant for drifting past tackles, attributes which have helped West Ham retain their Premiership status over the last two years.

Yet it looked for so long like Moncur wasn't going to make the grade in top flight football. Having joined Tottenham as an apprentice in 1984, he went on to make 21 appearances for the club. But even diehard Spurs fans can be forgiven for hardly remembering the 29-year-old Londoner. At an average of three per season, the appearances spanned a period of seven years!

"There were always great midfield players around at Tottenham, and always a few in the queue in front of me like Ardiles, Hoddle, Gascoigne, Stewart, Allen and Nayim, and I never really got a look in," he says. So eventually Moncur moved to Swindon in 1991.

"In a way, though, it was a good apprenticeship, because I got the chance to get a first hand look at a lot of good players. Glenn Hoddle is the best player I've ever seen in his position."

And it was his mentor that finally gave Moncur the chance to play a full season in the Premiership, signing him for the Swindon side that was taken over by John Gorman (where he was famously attacked by Eric Cantona in a vertical prelude to his Bruce Lee attack on Matthew Simmonds, a foul he says was "all part and parcel of the game").

It looked odds on that Moncur would follow Hoddle to Chelsea when Swindon went down, but instead it was the Hammers who came in for him. And he's only looked back since when there have been no options available for a killer ball forward.

John MONCUR

Age 34

Date of Birth 24.4.62

Place of Birth London

Nickname Psycho

League Games & Goals
Coventry 51 [4]
Nottingham Forest 368 [61]

Honours
League Cup 1989, 1990
FA Cup runners-up 1991

Transfers
Wealdstone to Coventry
(£25,000)
Coventry to Forest (£200,000)

Position/Role
Playing hard, looking hard

Did you know?
Stuart Pearce plays punk music at full volume before Forest games to wind himself and the rest of the team up

Word most often used to describe him
Psycho

Word never used to describe him
Softy

> "You have to play to your strengths and my strength is my strength."
>
> Stuart Pearce

tuart Pearce steps up and fires a 25-yard free-kick which flies into the top corner like an exocet missile. As his ecstatic team-mates jump for joy, Pearce trudges back to the half-way line with a face like Victor Meldrew. When Stuart Pearce is playing football there are plenty of thrills but no frills, he just gets on with being just about the best left back in the country. With Forest back in Europe and Pearce back in the England team – and captaining it against Bulgaria – the 34-year-old defender has found himself right back at the top, which is exactly where everyone at his first club, non-league Wealdstone FC, always knew he'd end up

"Stuart was always a special player," recalls Wealdstone's programme editor Roy Couch who watched most of his 200-plus appearances for the then Southern League outfit.

Bobby Gould noticed him too. It took the legendary star-of-the-future-spotter and then Coventry manager just eight minutes to make up his mind about signing him on a cold, wet night at Yeovil.

"Stuart was playing for Wealdstone," recalls Gould. "We'd driven half the day to get there and I was sat with my wife in the front row of the stand. After about eight minutes Stuart tackled the right winger who literally landed on my lap. That was all I needed to see and I got up to go. The wife couldn't believe it, she kept saying, 'But we've only been here eight minutes'."

But too many people confuse competitiveness with something more sinister when Stuart Pearce is on the pitch. In fact the Forest skipper has only been sent off twice in his whole career and one of those was for swearing. However tenaciously, he always goes for the ball, and though he can dish it out he can take it too.

And in an age when flashy forwards hone their skills on the springboard at their local baths and practice their goal celebrations in front of the mirror at home, there's nothing like a good, honest dose of Stuart Pearce. If he were ever to rip off his shirt, run to the corner flag and do an Elvis wiggle, English football might never recover.

Stuart PEARCE

Age 26

Date of Birth 12.2.70

Place of Birth Amsterdam

League games and goals
Ajax 103 [17]
Foggia 25 [11]
Forest 65 [21]

Brian Roy's 1995/96 season
Played in 28 of Forest's league games but will be disappointed with his measly eight goals, although he was troubled by injury, and having to play with Jason Lee…

Transfers
Foggia to Forest (£2.5m)

Position/Role
Zipping around, trying not to confuse Jason Lee too much

Word most often used to describe him
Nippy

Word never used to describe him
Lippy

> "As far as I'm concerned he's the best foreigner in Britain."
>
> Frank Clark

Maybe more people would take notice of Dutch star Bryan Roy if he copied Ruud Gullit and grew dreadlocks. Because the man with more tricks than Tommy Cooper, it seems, has found himself overshadowed by a couple of other Dutch players who have followed him into the Premiership. But even with Ruud Gullit and Dennis Bergkamp swelling the Dutch ranks in the Premier League, his boss Frank Clark is in no doubt who he'd prefer to be fighting the Forest cause.

"I could have signed Bergkamp," says Clark. "His agent rang us but I wasn't interested. Bryan is as good as there is in the position. He's more dangerous, he's got more pace and he can go past defenders with ease. As far as I'm concerned, he's the best foreigner in Britain."

Playing in the same deep attacking role that Bergkamp favours, Roy has been majestic for Forest over the past two seasons. Running at mesmerised defences and shooting on sight, at times he's played with the swagger of a true great. But at others, it has to be said, you've wondered if Forest's number 22 was still on the pitch at all.

All through his career Bryan Roy has been the genius who's yet to blossom. Stuck out on the wing at his first club Ajax, they said he'd never fulfil his potential and sold him to Italian club Foggia. At Foggia, given a free role in the middle of the field, he played the best football of his career but, whenever he pulled on the orange shirt of Holland, it didn't quite happen. He spent most of the 1994 World Cup on the bench and with the emergence of the likes of Patrick Kluivert and Marc Overmars he's hardly figured at international level since.

Quick footed, quick witted and damn, er, quick, he's got everything. If he could ever sustain his best form for a season or so, then we would be talking about a truly great footballer. Forest fans won't mind one bit if he hangs around for a couple more seasons on the off chance.

Bryan ROY

Age 32

Date of Birth 18.11.63

Place of Birth
Glodsone, Denmark

League Games & Goals
Brondby 214
Manchester United 190

Schmeichel's 1995/96 season
Conceded just 29 goals in 36 league matches. At home he let in just 9 all season. He even scored a goal with a header in the UEFA Cup!

Honours
Danish League [Brondby] 1987, 1988, 1989
Danish Cup 1989
Danish Player of the Year 1990
Rumbelows Cup 1992
FA Premiership 1992/93, 1993/94 and 1995/96
FA Cup 1994 and 1996
European Championship [Denmark] 1992

Transfers
Brondby to Man Utd (£550,000)

Position/Role
Looming large in front of the goal – at either end

Word most often used to describe him
Bright

Word never used to describe him
Meek

> "Schmeichel is the best in the world."
>
> Alex Ferguson

Peter Schmeichel's face turns from snowy white to fluorescent purple. He turns on Steve Bruce and proceeds to hurl a torrent of garbled Scandinavian abuse at the United skipper (Danish blue?). Why? The giant keeper's just sliced a goal kick straight into touch, that's why. Strange antics maybe, but like all great keepers Schmeichel doesn't exactly go in for your run of the mill rational behaviour.

"I don't care if he screams and bawls," claims Bruce (Alex Ferguson once said of the pair's on-field rows "they're like a couple of fishwives"). But Bruce reckons "it's his way of concentrating" and insists "Schmeichel is the best I've ever seen".

United fans wholeheartedly agree, and, since his bargain basement £550,000 move from Brondby in the summer of 1991, he's provided the rock-solid foundations for five years of United success. He's United's best ever keeper and that's official, statistics show he concedes on average one goal every 116 minutes.

How many times last season did the giant Dane keep United in a match? How often was a clean-through striker thwarted by Schmeichel's huge, fluorescent green frame? With hands the size of Jutland, an XXXL sized frame that swallows up the goal and the kind of super-confidence needed to dominate a Premiership penalty area, Schmeichel's got the lot.

But there's more to Schmeichel than shot stopping. With his colossal 'defence to attack' throws, which Alex Ferguson has described as "like Glenn Hoddle passes", it's like having another midfielder on the pitch. And then there's his goalscoring (as well as his UEFA Cup header against Rotor Volograd this season, he scored once in the Danish Third Division as well as in the 1994 Charity Shield penalty shoot-out against David Seaman).

In fact, he'd probably do a better job up front than Andy Cole, but Alex Ferguson knows that having Schmeichel between the sticks is one of the major reasons he's just stuck two big bits of silverware in the Old Trafford trophy cabinet.

Cantona might get the adulation while Giggsy and Sharpe get the groupies. Schmeichel just goes out and gets United results.

Peter SCHMEICHEL

Age 32

Date of Birth 19.9.63

Place of Birth Rotherham

League Games & Goals
Peterborough Utd 91
Birmingham City 75
QPR 141
Arsenal 227

David Seaman's 1995/96 season
Played in 38 of Arsenal's 42 games, conceding 31 goals

Honours
League Championship 1990/91
FA Cup 1993
League Cup 1993
European Cup Winners Cup 1994

Position/Role
Saving the day for Arsenal, usually

Word most often used to describe him
Safe

Word never used to describe him
Stylish

> "There's nothing better than knowing you're the best in the country."
>
> David Seaman

n the annals of football history it looks like David Seaman will be remembered for one thing. That goal he conceded when Nayim's 250-yard lob soared past his despairing grasp, lost Arsenal the 1995 Cup Winners' Cup and spawned a thousand Seaman jokes.

Every keeper has a bad day every now and again and, truth be told, it was the timing rather the nature of Seaman's misfortune that made that goal so memorable. It's a pity. In the semi-final of the same competition he made a save from a Lombardo penalty that had the country drooling with respect, and comparing him to Gordon Banks.

It's a goalkeeper's lot to be remembered for the bad moments, but for every one that England's number one has fallen prey to there have been a hundred blinding saves that will, in the long run, be forgotten. Seaman's problem, you could say, is that calmness and consistency are decideldly unspectacular... until it all goes wrong.

Nayim-hoofs apart, the slick haired Seaman has become the best English goalkeeper in the country. He is a great shot-stopper, with experience that lends a deal of anticipation to his razor-sharp reactions. His hands are as safe as houses when it comes to picking out crosses, and he's a great shouter who knows exactly how to organise his defence around him. What's more, he's a pretty shrewd distributor of the ball who doesn't have a panic attack and come out in a purple rash when it comes to his feet in a tight situation from an under pressure defender.

In short, he's the complete keeper, and one who has only finished on the losing side once in the (alas multicoloured) shirt of England, which he seems to have made his own. Or almost the complete keeper, as he proved when Nayim caught him off his line in Paris last spring. Still, Seaman makes fewer mistakes than (Schmeichel apart perhaps) any other goalkeeper in the Premiership.

To err is human, they say, which must make David Seaman some kind of robot. Then again, when he errs, he don't half err.

David SEAMAN

Age 26

Date of Birth 13.8.70

Place of Birth Newcastle

League Games & Goals
Southampton 118 [23]
Blackburn 140 [112]

Alan Shearer's 1995/96 season
Spent the season banging them in as usual, notching an astonishing 31 goals in 37 games. The rest of the team only managed 24 between them

Honours
FA Premiership 1994/5

Transfers
Southampton to Blackburn [£3.6m]

Did you know?
Last season, Alan Shearer scored no fewer than five hat-tricks, against Forest, Coventry, West Ham, Bolton and Tottenham

Position/Role
Blast 'em in for Blackburn, lay 'em off for England

Word most often used to describe him
Ruthless

Word never used to describe him
Chatty

> **"Goals are important to me. I've always got the number I've scored in the back of my mind."**
>
> Alan Shearer

f Alan Shearer could score goals for England as regularly as he thumps them in for Blackburn, he'd be playing for Milan by now. As it is, the Blackburn striker remains a bit of an enigma: deadly in the League, docile on the international front.

Or so the tabloids would have had it before Euro '96. During three glorious weeks in June, Shearer ended 12 barren matches for England, scoring 5 goals, to finish as the tournaments top scorer. By then the same tabloids believed him to be worth a cool £19m, if Blackburn could be forced to sell.

Shearer's strength is his strength. The 26-year-old Geordie is a thoroughly modern version of the typical old-fashioned English centre forward, and has a huge portfolio of swashbuckling goals to prove it.

"I've obviously been enormously impressed by Shearer and he's improving all the time," says England's last goalscoring hero Gary Lineker on the man who's hoping to replace him in the nation's hearts. "He's strong, he's determined, he's got a terrific shot, he's good in the air. OK, maybe he's not a great dribbler but all round his game is so strong and he knows where he's going."

Shearer actually has the potential to be better than Lineker, and England's second top goalscorer has admitted as much. "He's got a huge future. He's just got one final step to go, and that's to make it big at international level. He's got to learn new techniques, learn to play new kinds of defenders and systems but I'm sure he'll do it."

If Wor Alan's going to threaten Lineker's goal record for England, he's going to have to learn a bit more about the guile of foreign defenders. But learn he will, don't you worry. "You can learn off everyone and everything," he explains. "You can learn off watching the TV. If you can't learn then you won't go too far, will you? As I said, I'm still learning at 26 and I'm sure I'll be continuing to learn at 36."

If he finds out much more about Premiership defences, goalscoring records will start tumbling.

Alan SHEARER

Age 30

Date of Birth 2.4.66

Place of Birth
Highams Park

League Games & Goals
Millwall 220 [93]
Aldershot [loan] 4 [1]
Nottingham Forest 42 [14]
Tottenham Hotspur 137 [64]

Sheringham's 1995/96 season
Scored 16 goals in 38 league games, created rather more

Transfers
Millwall to Aldershot [loan]
Millwall to Nottm Forest [£2.0m]
Forest to Tottenham [£2.1m]

Position/Role
The unsung hero of Spurs and England

Word most often used to describe him
Complete

Word never used to describe him
Fast

> "Teddy Sheringham is a genuine all-round footballer."
>
> Garth Crooks

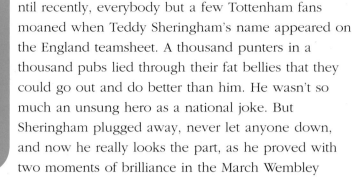

ntil recently, everybody but a few Tottenham fans moaned when Teddy Sheringham's name appeared on the England teamsheet. A thousand punters in a thousand pubs lied through their fat bellies that they could go out and do better than him. He wasn't so much an unsung hero as a national joke. But Sheringham plugged away, never let anyone down, and now he really looks the part, as he proved with two moments of brilliance in the March Wembley friendly against Bulgaria. The first was an exquisite turn and pass that would have graced the boot of a certain Glenn Hoddle and which sent Ferdinand free to score England's goal. The second, a venomous shot on the spin that needed a brilliant save from Mikhailov to prevent it from being the best England goal since Darren Anderton's 30-yard both-post-smacking thumper against Sweden in the Umbro Cup.

"He certainly deserves his place in the England team," says his Spurs skipper Gary Mabbutt, no stranger to the three lioned shirt himself and a man who suffers most days at the hands of his wily team-mate in training. "He's come on in leaps and bounds since he joined Tottenham, and he's improving all the time. The thing is many people don't notice half the work he's doing. His strength is his all-round ability."

Former Tottenham striker Garth Crooks agrees. "He's a genuine all-round footballer, which is an enormous strength. He doesn't just have the capacity to score goals, he can make them and he can stop them. And most importantly he has presence. A defence knows he's there and assumes respect. Martin Chivers had that sort of presence. Greaves had it, Best had it, Gascoigne has it, all the great players have it... It can give you an extra yard because you have respect."

Unlike pub punters and pompous pundits, Premiership defenders have been giving Sheringham respect for years: his 20-plus goals every season in the white shirt of Tottenham have made sure of that. Finally it looks like England fans are being forced to feel the same way. And about time too.

Teddy
SHERINGHAM

Age 28

Date of Birth 6.9.67

Place of Birth
Metkovic [Former Yugoslavia]

League Games & Goals
Dinamo Vinkovic [Former Yugoslavia]
Cadiz [Spain]
Hajduk Split [Croatia]
Derby County 28 [1]

Honours
Croatian League & Cup [1995]

Did you know?
Igor Stimac is Derby County's second most expensive player ever. He cost them £1.7m from Hajduk Split. He could have gone to Cologne in Germany or Vicenza in Italy but he chose Derby instead

Did you know?
Last season Derby had T-shirts saying 'Idemo Gore' printed on the front – Croation for 'going up'

Position/Role
Playing it cool when things get hot at the back

Word most often used to describe him
Classy

Word never used to describe him
Ungainly

"Derby County for me is a better place than Vicenza."

Igor Stimac

"Igor, Igor" shout the Baseball Ground faithful (to the, er, 'tune' of "Shearer, Shearer") whenever their Croatian international sweeper Igor Stimac does something good, which is rather often. They love Stimac at Derby, and they've every right to. The 28-year-old has been the missing part that has finally completed the promotion jigsaw, out of the Endsleigh League and into the Premiership.

Stimac plays the vital free man role in Derby's five strong defence, and it is his favourite position – he is usually forced into a full back berth for the Croatian national team. He is a defender in the style of Newcastle's Philippe Albert, an astute reader of the game who can play with the ball a bit. And at 6 foot 4ins he's no slouch in the air, either.

The classy defender, then, was a bit of a snip at £1.7m (if such a thing exists) although hardly any Derby fans had ever heard of him when he arrived at the club, with hardly a word of English in his head, back in November.

Stimac was rather well known in his home country, however, as skipper of the Hajduk Split team that had just won the Croatian league and cup double and had reached the quarter-finals of the European Cup, as well as an automatic choice for the national team that qualified at the top of its group, finishing ahead of Italy thanks to a famous victory in Palermo.

Derby's gain was Cologne and Vicenza's loss. Stimac liked the feel of the surroundings in the Midlands. "I can understand people's surprise that I should have signed for an Endsleigh League club in England," he said after the move. "The captain of our national side, Boban, plays for Milan, others play for Barcelona and Lazio. But it is important to feel comfortable where you are living, especially when you have a family."

The Endsleigh League looks a long way away now, as Derby prepare for life in the top flight. Stimac is confident about the future. "As captain of Hajduk I achieved a lot of success and I don't see why that should change at Derby," he says. Success for the Rams this season would be Premiership survival, but you get the feeling that Stimac will thrive.

Igor STIMAC

Age 25

Date of Birth 10.8.71

Place of Birth Gateshead

Nickname Stoney

League Games & Goals
Nottingham Forest 133 [18]

Steve Stone's 1995/96 season
Apart from taking the international scene by storm for England [scoring twice, against Switzerland and Portugal] played 34 league games for Forest and scored 7 times.

Position/Role
Rolling past defenders

Word most often used to describe him
Bald

Word never used to describe him
Flash

> "When you grow up in Newcastle there's not much else you want to do except be a footballer."
>
> Steve Stone

When Steve Stone suddenly found himself thrust into the England limelight, he found it tough. It's not that he found the jump from club football to international status easy to bridge, far from it; it's just that he had to tell his girlfriend Judith that their wedding – arranged for right in the middle of the European Championships – might have to be postponed.

Stone's meteoric surge on to the international scene took everyone by surprise, none more so than the man himself. But after impressing in his first appearance as sub against Norway, Stone scored in his next two games against Switzerland and Portugal and was named man of the match in both. Suddenly England had a new star.

For the 24-year-old from Gateshead who looks, er, slightly older ("even my mum's bald" he once joked of his family) it's all a long way from the years he spent fighting injury as a Forest reserve when he broke his leg no fewer than three times. "Brian Clough saw me hobbling around on crutches one day and said: 'Bugger off home and don't come back until you're off those bloody things'."

He remembers spending more time cleaning boots than showing defenders a clean pair of heels, but his patience was rewarded when Frank Clark began to realise that he might have a more precious Stone on his hands than he'd first realised.

Switched on to the Forest flank almost by accident after the arrival of Lars Bohinen, Stone realised he needed to learn a few tricks and start taking players on if he was going to make it at the City Ground. The rest is history.

And with a wise, albeit thinning, head on his shoulders, Steve Stone isn't likely to let his career start rolling backwards. His manager, Frank Clark, believes he's likely to get even better.

"Before Steve got in the England side we were of the opinion that he was much better suited to the quick, hurly burly English tempo than the more thoughtful European scene," says Clark. "But he's improved so much as a player, especially with England, and there's no limit to what he can achieve."

Steve STONE

Age 24

Date of Birth 31.10.71

Place of Birth Watford

League Games & Goals
Oxford 2
Spurs 126

Ian Walker's 1995/96 season
Played in every single one of Tottenham's 38 league games, plus all the cup games, too. In the league he conceded 36 goals.

International career
Forced himself into the England reckoning last season, earning himself a regular place on the bench as understudy for David Seaman and Tim Flowers

Position/Role
Safe hands, silly haircut

Did you know?
Ian Walker posed nude for a womans magazine in the White Hart Lane changing rooms.

Word most often used to describe him
Safe

Word never used to describe him
Manic

> ## "Ian's the same as me, I never get too excited."
> ### Mike Walker

t's been said of too many promising young goalkeepers, but I'm going to say it again. Ian Walker looks like he could well be the England keeper for years to come, when he finally displaces David Seaman from the number 1 spot. And the main reason isn't to do with his considerable physical prowess: it's all in his head.

One man who, not surprisingly, agrees is another former professional goalkeeper – and more famously, Premiership manager – Mike Walker, his dad.

"Ian's positional play and his handling are very strong," says the former Norwich and Everton man. "They have been from an early age: and I'm talking six or seven. But his main strength is his temperament, which is very good. You look at all the best goalkeepers of the past: like Banks, like Jennings, like Shilton, and they've all had very good composure. Ian's the same. Maybe it's rubbed off from me a bit, I never get too excited."

Walker Jnr certainly has had many experienced keepers in close proximity to coach him. "He's been very lucky," says Walker Snr. "When he arrived at Tottenham Ray Clemence was there, and now Pat Jennings is at White Hart Lane as goalkeeping coach. And Mike Kelly was a big influence when he trained at the Lilleshall School of Excellence when he was a kid."

The 6 foot 1ins keeper isn't far off being a kid now; he's still just 24, though you wouldn't think it when you look back on a career that started in 1990. This is the first full season he's had at Tottenham though, having finally wrested the green (and yellow and pink and blue) jersey from the enormously experienced Norwegian international Eric Thorsvedt. "His next step is to get into the England team," says his father. "He's always been adamant from an early age that that's what he wants to do. And he's a determined man. It's a calm determination, which is often confused for a lack of passion. Nothing could be further from the truth."

As a parting shot I ask Dad Walker if his son has any weaknesses. To my surprise he gives me an answer. "Maybe he could stand up a little more," he says, semi cryptically. Premiership strikers take note: hear it from a man who knows.

Ian WALKER

Age 29

Date of Birth 15.12.66

Place of Birth Kensington

League Games & Goals
Wimbledon 135 [27]
Chelsea 187 [40]

Dennis Wise's 1995/96 season
Figured in 35 of Chelsea's 38 league games, and notched 7 goals

Honours
FA Cup 1988 (Wimbledon)

Transfers
Wimbledon to Chelsea [£1.6m]

Position/Role
Letting his feet do the talking, thank goodness

Word most often used to describe him
Shorty

Word(s) never used to describe him
Big man

> "I like playing with Dennis Wise very much, he's a good player."
>
> Ruud Gullitt

 tall, dark Dutchman with dreadlocks may have been hogging the limelight in Chelsea's midfield this season...but a short, pasty skinhead by the name of Dennis Wise has been revelling in Ruud Gullit's shadow. For while the footballing world drools over Gullit's masterful ability, he of the cheeky grin and high-pitched voice has grown in stature alongside his Dutch master. But Wise's midfield performances haven't gone completely unnoticed, and during Terry Venables' reign he was a squad regular.

Now skipper of a Chelsea side looking forward to pastures new (yet again) and playing the best football of his life, it's all a long way from being rejected by Southampton for being too small. It was then that he was picked up on a 'free' by Wimbledon where he became the arch provider for arch finisher John Fashanu. In Wimbledon's 1987/88 FA Cup winning year, he was the provider or scorer of no fewer than 75 per cent of the Dons' goals.

A £1.6 million move to Chelsea followed before the 1990/91 season and, despite the occasional disciplinary blemish – both on and off the pitch – he's been just about Chelsea's most consistent player (albeit over five years of miserable inconsistency).

Wise combines tough-tackling and hard-running with supreme natural skill and ball control, the ability to pick out passes which even Gullit would be proud of, and a dead ball expertise for which he has few rivals in the Premiership.

If Wise is ever to make the step from excellent Premiership player to one of true international standing – which, make no mistake, is within his ability – then perhaps what he really needs is a decent team around him. With Gullitt at the helm this is surely his, and Chelsea's, best chance in years to do just that. But then we seem to have been saying that about the Blues since the early 1970s.

If Chelsea ever do start to really tick, though, you can bet your last tube of hair gel that little Dennis Wise will be right at the heart of it.

Dennis WISE

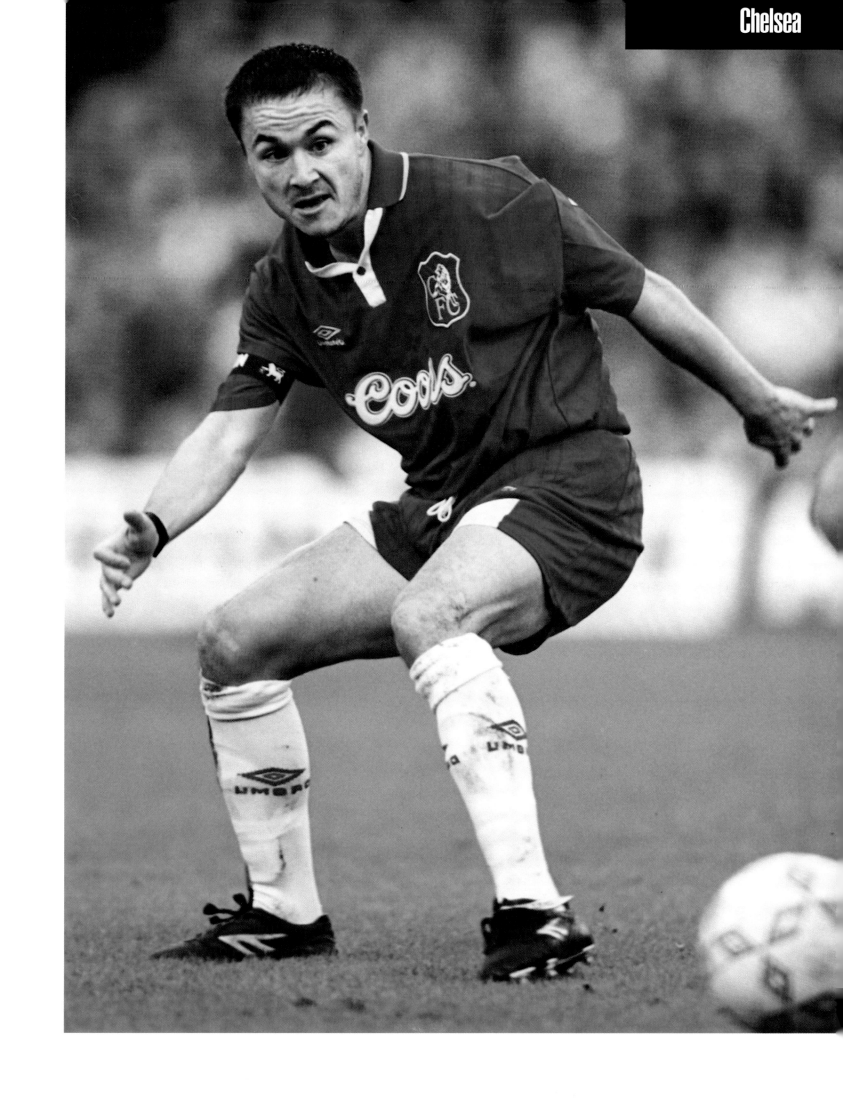

Age 32

Date of Birth 3.11.63

Place of Birth Woolwich

League Games & Goals
Crystal Palace 225 [90]
Arsenal 162 [75]

Ian Wright's 1995/96 season
Wright hit 15 goals in 31 league games for the Gunners

Honours
Coca Cola Cup 1993,
FA Cup 1993

Transfers
Greenwich Boro to Palace [free]
Palace to Arsenal [£2.5m]

Position/Role
Impressing us mere mortals

Did you know?
Ian Wright has a tattoo of a Harley Davidson motorbike on his right thigh!

Word most often used to describe him
Fiery

Word never used to describe him
Shy

"To score a goal that ordinary people couldn't score is what you have to aim for."

Ian Wright

New York may be so good they named it twice, but Ian Wright is so good he goes one better. 'Ian Wright, Wright, Wright' is a one-man scoring machine. With his heart on his sleeve, his emotions always on the boil and the ball invariably nestling in the Highbury net, his name has become synonymous with scoring goals for Arsenal.

Which is why the famous London club was rocked to its foundations last season when Wright demanded a transfer after a bust-up with Gunners' boss Bruce Rioch. Wright claimed he felt he didn't fit into Rioch's plans, and the Arsenal Chairman Sir Peter Hill-Wood was quoted as saying, "I will be sad to see him go", and that, it seemed, was that.

Then, a few weeks later, Wright backed down, claiming he never wanted to leave, that Arsenal was in his blood and that he wanted to stay and finish his career at Highbury.

Whatever twists and turns will befall Wright next, whether he stays at Arsenal, signs for Chelsea, Everton or Dumbarton, you can be sure he'll give his all for the cause. At 32 he might be getting on a bit, but the fire still rages ferociously inside his belly and, let's face it, if you were a defender you wouldn't want to face him.

Signed from Palace in 1991, Wright has done more than anyone since then to explode the 'boring, boring Arsenal' myth. And although there's so much more to his game than sticking the ball in the onion bag, it's his thirst for goalscoring glory that drives him on.

"All I see at the end of the season is the golden boot," he says. "That's what I go for, and I know if I score enough goals at the end of the season I'll get that. I'd rather score two goals from tap-ins than one that's a bit special, but I must say I do love scoring spectacular goals. To score a goal that ordinary people won't be able to score is what you have to aim for."

Wrighty has scored a few of those and, without doubt, he'll score a few more, but will it be in the red shirt of Arsenal? Fifty thousand Gooners will have had their fingers – and other parts of their anatomies – crossed all summer.

Ian WRIGHT

Age 30

Date of Birth 6.6.66

Place of Birth Ghana

League Games & Goals
Saarbrucken
[Germany] 65 [26]
Eintracht Frankfurt
[Germany] 123 [68]
Leeds 40 [25]

Tony Yeboah's 1995/96 season
Scored 12 goals in 22 games in a season interrupted by injury and the African Nations Cup. Started the campaign like a wild puma, winning the Goal of the Month award twice in a row, but tailed off towards the end of the campaign

Position/Role
Professional Goal of the Month winner

Word most often used to describe him
Spectacular

Word[s] never used to describe him
Brian Deane

> "Yeboah is a cross between Pele and Carl Lewis."
>
> Franz Beckenbauer

Not so long ago, Leeds boss Howard Wilkinson was watching satellite TV, when he noticed an African playing in Germany for Eintracht Frankfurt by the name of Tony Yeboah who scored goals for fun. When he heard that Yeboah was in dispute with the club, he snapped him up, and Premiership football hasn't quite been the same since.

Now, in playground-speak, to score a 'Yeboah' is just about the best thing you can do. The Ghanaian international, it seems, hardly bothers scoring unless it's going to be a corker.

"He's an out and out goal scorer," said his skipper Gary McAllister before the 1995/6 season. "But it's the way he puts the ball in the net that's interesting. I don't think he blasted one in all season. He lets the keeper make the first move, and then lifts it over him or slots it past him. He passes it into the goal."

Yeboah must have read his captain's words, and as soon as the new season started he volleyed them right down his throat again. The Match of the Day, August Goal of the Month Award could have been renamed "Yeboah of the Month" with two goals that were out of this world, a half volley on the turn against Liverpool, and another against Wimbledon where he beat two men, scooped the ball up, kneed it into the air, and smashed it past Paul Heald via the underside of the bar. Even Alan Hansen didn't blame the defence for that one.

Even though Leeds went off the boil pretty quickly last season (with Yeboah missing a number of games through injury or international duty), Leeds fans were delighted that he recently signed a new contract for the Yorkshire club until 1998, after which he has said he will retire from the game. Yeboah signed because he was in love with Leeds, because he was in love with Yorkshire pud, and because he was in love with Premiership defences.

"English defences are usually flat," he says, "which gives the striker an advantage. In Germany when I beat someone there was usually a sweeper. In England with my speed I make it difficult for anyone to get back to cover." For English stoppers, 1998 can't come soon enough.

Tony YEBOAH

Age 25

Date of Birth 3.11.71

Place of Birth Tobago

League Games & Goals
Aston Villa 163 [44]

Dwight Yorke's 1995/96 season
His best by miles, scoring 17 goals in 35 league games and finally fulfilling that immense potential

Honours
1996 Coca Cola Cup

Did you know?
Apart from Brian Lara, Dwight Yorke's best friend is Newcastle goalkeeper Shaka Hislop

Did you know?
Villa fans sing 'It's up to you Dwight Yorke' to the tune of 'New York, New York'

Position/Role
Putting a smile on Brian Little's face

Word most often used to describe him
Improved

Word never used to describe him
Conventional

> "My mum hated football. She used to shout at me to come in, I had to run and hide in the park."
>
> Dwight Yorke

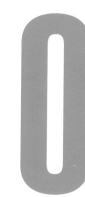ne moment last season summed up the precocious, exciting, cheeky-chappy nature of Trinidadian international Dwight Yorke's footballing style. It was the FA Cup Fourth Round and Aston Villa were playing Sheffield United at Bramall Lane. The score was 0-0, and Villa were struggling to contain Howard Kendall's revamped side, already cup conquerors of Arsenal. Milosevic went down, the ref blew for a penalty, and Yorke elected to take it. Did he side-foot it into the corner or blast it to beat keeper Alan Kelly for pace? Did he hell! He anticipated that Kelly would dive and sweetly chipped it to where the keeper had been standing, right in the middle of the goal, about an inch below the bar. Of course Kelly fell for it and the ball gently arced into the net.

Yorke would have looked pretty dumb if the keeper had stood his ground. As it was he got away with the risk and had every football fan in the country breathless with admiration the next day. It was typical of the Yorke's unconventional derring-do style, which has seen him become the most exciting player on Villa's books.

His admirers include David Platt, a Villa player when Graham Taylor paid a mere £180,000 to bring Yorke to Villa from his native Tobago in the West Indies. "Now Dwight's having a lengthy run in the side he's fulfilling his potential," says the England captain. "At such a young age it's frightening how good he can become."

It could so easily have been cricket that Yorke was getting good at. Great mates with Brian Lara he was a handy wicket keeper and quite a nifty batsman too. But at 17 he was offered the chance to play for the Trinidad national team, and has never looked back. And although it's his can't-guess-what-the-hell-he's-going-to-do-next trickery that makes him catch the eye at Villa, Yorke admits he's not there yet. "I've got to keep learning. To better myself as a person and a player," he says.

Dwight Yorke: nice guy, great player. The future looks frightening.

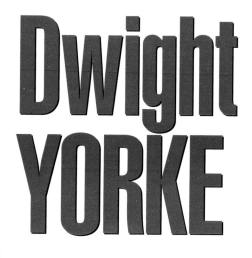

Dwight YORKE

Predictions for the

W ith 760 matches to be played in the Premiership this season, you'd need Russell Grant, Uri Geller and half a ton of computer equipment to work out how the League table might look at the end of the season. Russell Grant's too expensive, Uri Geller's too temperamental and we can't afford any computers, so we sat down with a cup of tea and a packet of custard creams and worked it out for ourselves instead...

Predicted final table 1996/97

1 Liverpool	6 Tottenham	11 Chelsea	16 Sheffield Wed
2 Manchester Utd	7 Arsenal	12 West Ham	17 Sunderland
3 Newcastle Utd	8 Middlesbrough	13 Notts Forest	18 Derby County
4 Blackburn Rovers	9 Everton	14 Coventry	19 Southampton
5 Aston Villa	10 Leeds	15 Wimbledon	20 Leicester City

Liverpool

Prediction 1st

Liverpool are no longer a team of kids and we reckon that this is going to be their year. Roy Evans has started doing things the Liverpool way again and his quiet revolution has produced a well-balanced side capable of bulldozing aside the smaller clubs in the Premiership and winning the crunch matches to boot. In Collymore and Fowler he has the best strike force in the land, which is almost certainly getting better. McManaman, in his free-roving role, can terrify the calmest of defences with his probing runs, and the five-man defence is well capable of mopping up pressure and turning defence quickly into attack. The good days are back again at Anfield.

Manchester United

Prediction 2nd

Alex Ferguson's bunch have become the team everyone loves to hate and the reason is envy. Having won the Double twice and three of the last four Premiership titles nobody's going to be betting very much against them topping the Premier League again. Eric Cantona is their heart, and when the going gets tough he quickens the pulse, seemingly able to score that crucial goal at will. Ryan Giggs has matured from whizzkid to complete footballer and the likes of Beckham, Scholes and the Neville brothers are getting better every game. But with a place in the Champions League they'll be hard pressed to keep up their league form whilst battling on all four fronts.

Newcastle United

Prediction 3rd

The hysteria and disappointment that surrounded Newcastle's run-in to the end of the season last year may have one of two effects: it might crush the spirit of Keegan's players or it might fire them up to try again harder still. The main problem Keegan's team had throughout the season was their defensive naiveté: however once Elliot and Watson had taken over at full-back from the more flamboyant Barton and Beresford, Newcastle looked tighter and only conceded two goals in their last five games. If they can ally this new-found solidity with their usual attacking flair, they could go far. Perhaps their best chance however lies in winning one of the cups.

PREMIER LEAGUE

Top Attendances

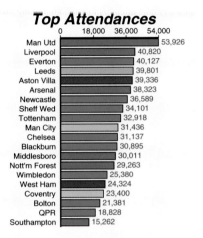

Man Utd	53,926
Liverpool	40,820
Everton	40,127
Leeds	39,801
Aston Villa	39,336
Arsenal	38,323
Newcastle	36,589
Sheff Wed	34,101
Tottenham	32,918
Man City	31,436
Chelsea	31,137
Blackburn	30,895
Middlesboro	30,011
Nott'm Forest	29,263
Wimbledon	25,380
West Ham	24,324
Coventry	23,400
Bolton	21,381
QPR	18,828
Southampton	15,262

0   18,000   36,000   54,000

Yellow & Red Cards

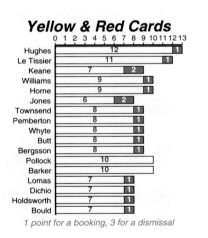

0 1 2 3 4 5 6 7 8 9 10 11 12 13

Hughes	12 1
Le Tissier	11 1
Keane	7 2
Williams	9 1
Horne	9 1
Jones	6 2
Townsend	8 1
Pemberton	8 1
Whyte	8 1
Butt	8 1
Bergsson	8 1
Pollock	10
Barker	10
Lomas	7 1
Dichio	7 1
Holdsworth	7 1
Bould	7 1

1 point for a booking, 3 for a dismissal

Lowest Gates

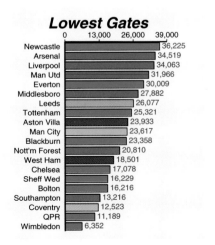

0   13,000   26,000   39,000

Newcastle	36,225
Arsenal	34,519
Liverpool	34,063
Man Utd	31,966
Everton	30,009
Middlesboro	27,882
Leeds	26,077
Tottenham	25,321
Aston Villa	23,933
Man City	23,617
Blackburn	23,358
Nott'm Forest	20,810
West Ham	18,501
Chelsea	17,078
Sheff Wed	16,229
Bolton	16,216
Southampton	13,216
Coventry	12,523
QPR	11,189
Wimbledon	6,352

Blackburn

Prediction 4th

The legacy of Kenny Dalglish's abrupt departure from champions Blackburn before last season was a disastrous start on all fronts. The world and his wife doubted Ray Harford's ability as a manager, and despite having the best striker in the league, Blackburn struggled into Christmas. As spring approached, however, Blackburn started to look devastating, especially at Ewood Park. It would take a fool to write them off this season.

Tottenham Hotspur

Prediction 6th

Tottenham will have to become more consistent if they want to stop being a side that challenges for a UEFA spot and is dangerous in the cups and start becoming serious title contenders. They proved last season that on their day they can be one of the best sides in the country (remember that 4-1 win over Manchester United?). But Gerry Francis needs to strengthen his squad if he wants to get back into the big league.

Middlesbrough

Prediction 8th

After an autumn climb to the heels of the title runners, Middlesbrough went into freefall last term and, if the season had lasted a couple of weeks more, would surely have gone down. Manager Bryan Robson suffered more than his fair share of injuries, sure, but at this level needs more talent in his squad to make sure that Middlesbrough can keep in the safety of a mid-table position.

Aston Villa

Prediction 5th

Just over a year ago, new manager Brian Little was staring the Endsleigh League in its ugly face. But Villa will start 1996/7 with aspirations of winning the title and looking forward to a European campaign. Villa are very tight defensively and deadly on the break. They should have few problems winning consistently against the middle order clubs: their progress will depend on whether or not they can start regularly beating the big boys.

Arsenal

Prediction 7th

Last-gasp qualification for Europe meant that Arsenal could, at least, gain satisfaction from realising they'd achieved as much out of the season as Newcastle. They scarcely deserved to – despite the presence of such international stars as Dennis Bergkamp, David Platt, Tony Adams and (er) Glenn Helder, but this year it can only get better. If it doesn't, they might have to bring back George Graham.

Everton

Prediction 9th

Funny old team, Everton. Everyone who supports them insists so often they are 'a big club' that you can tell they're afraid that they aren't so big after all any more. They have the grit and determination to cause problems to any side they face, but are equally prone to falling apart at the seams at the drop of a blue and white bobble hat. They are too good to go down, but probably not good enough to gain a place in Europe. A nice cup run this season might cheer up the folk living the wrong side of Stanley Park.

Leeds

Prediction 10th

Sure, Alex Ferguson's 'cheats' accusations at the end of last season was an obvious exercise in kidology: but his words did have a ring of truth about them. On paper, Leeds looked fabulous. On the pitch, it was all too often a different proposition. Chock full of quality players – McAllister, Speed, Yeboah, Kelly – Leeds simply failed to work well enough as a unit to offer enough consistency to challenge for a place in Europe. It appears that it's the team's morale, rather than its playing staff, that needs strengthening.

Chelsea

Prediction 11th

Is there life after Glenn Hoddle? The new England manager spent three years crafting a well balanced and skilful unit from a pig's ear, signed one of the world's best players, and steered a seemingly mediocre side to an FA Cup Final, a Cup Winners' Cup semi and another FA Cup semi. Can Ruud Gullit carry on where St. Glenda left off? A great deal depends on whether or not he can keep the side playing in the same quick-moving, short-passing manner. Wholesale changes at this point would be disastrous (although Vialli's presence will be welcomed), and could ruin a great deal of hard work. Otherwise Europe beckons.

West Ham

Prediction 12th

Harry Redknapp's side were widely tipped for relegation before last season kicked off, but, after a dodgy start, actually finished in a comfortable pipe-and-slippers midfield position, 13 points clear of relegation. Such is the state of English football at the moment that most Hammers fans would be happy with a rerun, and, such is the state of English football at the moment that they'll almost certainly get it. They shouldn't find too much trouble amassing points against the also-rans, but will find it hard to beat the big boys often enough to be involved in the UEFA Cup scrap. They could do without the dodgy start, this time round, mind.

Nottingham Forest

Prediction 13th

Most people will remember Nottingham Forest last season for their pooping of the title run-in party by getting thrashed by Man Utd and then stealing two points off Newcastle. Why did Ian Woan have to go and score that goal? Forest have some good individual players, and can play some sparkling football, but let their heads go down too often when the going gets tough. This is the side, remember, that let a 2-0 lead at Anfield turn into a 4-2 defeat, and got stuffed home and away by Blackburn Rovers. They'll need to pull those red socks right up if they don't want a relegation battle on their hands this time round.

Coventry

Prediction 14th

Another escape act worthy of the great Paul Daniels (well aren't you sick of that Houdini cliché?) sees Coventry start their 30th consecutive campaign in the top flight: but it's difficult to see them getting anywhere near their best ever position – sixth in 1969/70. Truth be told, though, the Sky Blues have a talented side that would have shone out a few years ago when general standards were lower, and, though you can't see them do more this season than maybe getting a little cup run together, Big Ron should easily be able to steer them to safety.

Wimbledon

Prediction 15th

Standards have risen recently, which means that Wimbledon's traditonal shoestring cut-and-thrustmanship doesn't slash quite as much mustard as it used to. On the other hand, if you bottled the Crazy Gang spirit you could sell if for millions and Sam Hammam's wiliness makes the club one of the most successful small businesses in London. But without enough money to compete in the flair-buying stakes, Wimbledon will once again have to rely on their ability to give better teams a damn good fright if they are to stay in the Premiership.

Top League Scorers

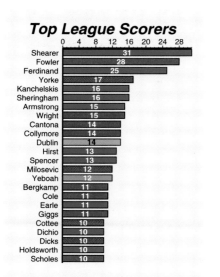

Shearer	31
Fowler	28
Ferdinand	25
Yorke	17
Kanchelskis	16
Sheringham	16
Armstrong	15
Wright	15
Cantona	14
Collymore	14
Dublin	14
Hirst	13
Spencer	13
Milosevic	12
Yeboah	12
Bergkamp	11
Cole	11
Earle	11
Giggs	11
Cottee	10
Dichio	10
Dicks	10
Holdsworth	10
Scholes	10

When all Bookings occurred

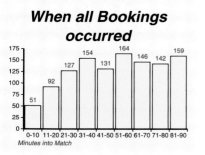

Minutes into Match	
0-10	51
11-20	92
21-30	127
31-40	154
41-50	131
51-60	164
61-70	146
71-80	142
81-90	159

Dismissals by Club

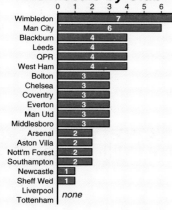

Wimbledon	7
Man City	6
Blackburn	4
Leeds	4
QPR	4
West Ham	4
Bolton	3
Chelsea	3
Coventry	3
Everton	3
Man Utd	3
Middlesboro	3
Arsenal	2
Aston Villa	2
Nott'm Forest	2
Southampton	2
Newcastle	1
Sheff Wed	1
Liverpool	none
Tottenham	none

When all Goals have been scored

Minutes into Match	
0-10	84
11-20	97
21-30	93
31-40	90
41-50	114
51-60	122
61-70	133
71-80	113
81-90	142

Sheffield Wednesday

Prediction 16th

The one consolation for Sheffield Wed fans at the moment is that, unlike during the 1970s and 1980s, at least this giant is slumbering in the top flight. Well they are for the time being. A humdrum nondescript season ended with a free-fall that could have seen the Yorkshire club relegated on the last day of the season. They'll need to put a little more steel into their performances to stop the rot at the beginning of this term. It will take something really special to get this club back on the right tracks – an ageing attack needs to be replaced and a leaky defence to be patched up just to stay in the top flight.

Derby

Prediction 18th

It's taken Derby County five years to get back into the top flight after relegation in 1991, so it won't please their fans too much to see them being predicted right back into the Endsleigh League. But although they have some good young players (look out for midfielder Matt Carbon), a handful of seasoned pros (remember Marco Gabbiadini?) and a couple of cultured foreigners (Igor Stimac is a regular in the Croatia team), fighting against relegation has become such an art form in recent years that the experience is likely to prove conclusive. Let's hope the Rams enjoy their trip, though.

Southampton

Prediction 19th

The sad truth is that Southampton aren't quite rich enough to happily keep their top-flight status, and this season could well be their last for some time in the Premier League, especially after an exodus of first team players has left them looking increasingly thin on the ground. A last-gasp 0-0 draw at home to Wimbledon saw them stay up on goal difference last season. Many of their fans may be wishing that the Dons had put them out of their misery as this term progresses. Mind you they'll still beat Newcastle at the Dell. It's become a tradition.

Sunderland

Prediction 17th

The ever-widening gulf between the Endsleigh League and the Premiership means that it is increasingly difficult for promoted clubs to stay up, and Sunderland will undoubtedly struggle in the Premier League. They had the chance to show off a bit with a couple of home games after their early promotion from Division One last season, but didn't manage a goal in either game which will worry manager Peter Reid a little, and, Maccam fans hope, have him reaching out for his cheque book. Nobody will fancy travelling to Roker Park, though, and that should see them scrape home.

Leicester City

Prediction 20th

If Leicester City carry on like this they'll have to re-name them Yo-Yo City. Now they're up again, but for how long? Chances are they'll be straight down again unless someone gives Martin O'Neil a brown paper bag with £10 million in it. Even that might not be enough. The gap between the Premiership and the Endsleigh is bigger than ever and Leicester didn't even look a particularly strong First Division outfit last season. Still, with Martin O'Neill's legendary motivation skills and a couple of new signings, they might just survive. But it's a big 'might'.

1995/96 Premier

Top 10 Goalscorers

Alan Shearer	31
Robbie Fowler	28
Les Ferdinand	25
Dwight Yorke	17
Teddy Sheringham	16
Ian Wright	15
Chris Armstrong	15
Eric Cantona	14
Stan Collymore	14
Tony Yeboah	12

Top 10 'Providers'

Steve McManaman (assists)	25
Ryan Giggs	17
Dwight Yorke	17
Andy Cole	16
Eric Cantona	16
Stan Collymore	15
Keith Gillespie	14
Trevor Sinclair	14
Matt Le Tissier	14
Ian Woan	13

10 clubs with most away wins

Man Utd	10
Newcastle Utd	7
Aston Villa	7
Arsenal	7
Everton	7
Tottenham	7
Liverpool	6
Chelsea	5
West Ham	5
Wimbledon	5

Top 10 'Leaky defences'

Bolton (conceded)	71
Wimbledon	70
Sheffield Wednesday	61
Coventry	60
Man City	58
QPR	57
Leeds	57
Nottm Forest	54
West Ham	52
Southampton	52

Top 10 'High scoring teams'

Man Utd	73
Liverpool	70
Newcastle	66
Everton	64
Blackburn	61
Wimbledon	55
Aston Villa	52
Tottenham	50
Nottm Forest	50
Arsenal	49

Top 10 'draw' specialists

Chelsea	14
Coventry	14
Nottm Forest	13
Tottenham	13
Arsenal	12
Liverpool	11
Man City	11
Southampton	11
Wimbledon	11
Everton	10

2 players sent off more than once

Vinny Jones v Liverpool [h]	
(later reduced to yellow card)	
v Forest [a]	
v Chelsea [a]	
Roy Keane v Forest [a]	
v Middlesbrough [h]	

5 seriously big wins

Blackburn	7	Nottm Forest	1
Bolton	0	Man Utd	6
Newcastle	6	Wimbledon	1
Sheff Wed	2	Everton	5
Nottm Forest	7	Sheff Wed	1

Top 10 Silly Haircuts

Jason Lee	('He's got a pineapple...')
Barry Venison	(Highlights on Sky)
Danny Dichio	(Nearly as silly as the sideburns)
Ray Parlour	(Beach bum)
Darren Peacock	(Too much too long)
Ian MacGregor	(Supergrass copy)
Mark Crossley	(Bubble perm man)
Eric Cantona	(Foreign legion look)
John Beresford	(Warren Barton lookalike)
Warren Barton	(John Beresfod lookalike)

League Stats

Top 10 penalty scoring teams

West Ham	5
Everton	4
Man Utd	4
Middlesbrough	4
Southampton	4
Arsenal	3
Bolton	3
Newcastle	3
Nottm Forest	3
Aston Villa	2

10 great Premiership hat-tricks

Alan Shearer (five)	v	Coventry	[Sept 23rd, Ewood Park]
	v	Forest	[Nov 18th, Ewood Park]
	v	West Ham	[Dec 2nd, Ewood Park]
	v	Bolton	[Feb 3rd, Ewood Park]
	v	Tottenham	[Mar 16th, White Hart Lane]
Robbie Fowler (three)	v	Bolton	[Sep 23rd, Anfield]
	v	Arsenal	[Dec 23rd, Anfield]
	v	Forest	[Jan 1st, Anfield]
Les Ferdinand (two)	v	Wimbledon	[Oct 21st, St James' Park]
	v	Wimbledon	[Dec 3rd, Selhurst Park]

Top 10 clubs with the most home wins

Newcastle	17
Man Utd	15
Liverpool	14
Blackburn	14
Aston Villa	11
Nottm Forest	11
Arsenal	10
Everton	10
Tottenham	9
West Ham	9

5 goals scored in the 1st minute

Dwight Yorke (Aston Villa v Coventry)	13 secs
Ryan Giggs (Man Utd v Southampton	16 secs
John Ebbrell (Wimbledon v Everton)	28 secs
Ian Dowie (West Ham v Middlesbrough	40 secs
Mixu Paatelainen (Bolton v Everton)	45 secs

Top 10 scorers of the most headers

Wimbledon	22
Aston Villa	18
Coventry	17
Newcastle	16
Tottenham	16
Everton	14
Bolton	13
Leeds	13
Man Utd	13
Blackburn	12

Top 10 dead ball specialists

Wimbledon (goals)	20
West Ham	16
Southampton	14
Arsenal	12
Liverpool	12
Man Utd	12
Blackburn	10
Everton	10
Leeds	10
Tottenham	10

Index